I0753003

For those who came before us and those who follow — we're just a link in a chain that won't be broken.

The Last Ones of Auschwitz
By Sophie Nahum & Leslie Gelrubin Benitah
Copyright © 2025 Hello Prod
ISBN: 979-8-9936186-0-9
All rights reserved.

The Auschwitz Album : pp. 130, 135, 168, 192
Shelomo Selinger drawings : pp. 143, 182, 186, 198
Most of the photos come from the personal collections of the witnesses and from The Last Ones project (Xavier Liberman). Photos of Nazi perpetrators are used here for educational and historical purposes and are not subject to copyright to the best of our knowledge.

No part of this publication may be reproduced, distributed, or transmitted in any form or by any means, including photocopying, recording, or other electronic or mechanical methods, without the prior written permission of the publisher, except as permitted by U.S. copyright law. For permission requests, contact Hello Prod: laurentpreece@helloprodllc.com.

Editor: Laurent Preece / Hello Prod
Book Cover & Design: Fernand Dutilleux
Iconography: Bob Rayers
Typesetting: Plaak 2 Griffon (205.tf), Martina Plantijn (Klim Type Foundry), Söhne (Klim Type Foundry)
Publisher: Hello Prod

Sophie Nahum
Leslie Gelrubin Benitah

THE LAST ONES OF AUSCHWITZ

Encounters with Auschwitz Survivors

(Preface)

HOW IT ALL STARTED?

Sophie and Leslie tell you the story behind The last ones project

Leslie: What made you want to start this mission—visiting survivors, collecting their stories, and sharing them with the world?

Sophie: It's a long story—but really, it started with one man named Jacques Altmann.

I'm not a direct descendant of Holocaust survivors. I didn't grow up with that weight at home, so It wasn't taboo for me. My grandparents were from North Africa, they had to leave with nothing, just suitcases and four kids, but it wasn't something we were told not to talk about and I've spent my entire childhood asking them about their past.

The first time I ever met a Holocaust survivor was in 2010, while making a documentary about Victor Young Perez—a Jewish boxing world champion who ended up in Auschwitz, forced to fight in the camp for Nazi entertainment. That's when I met Jacques Altmann, one of the last people who knew him. He was 88 at the time—today he's 102. And it hit me.

These survivors won't be around much longer. My future children won't ever meet them.

So I thought—we need to build a bridge. A human, emotional link between the last witnesses and the next generation.

At first, I didn't even know how to speak to someone who'd survived Auschwitz. I thought, I thought, should you bow? But Jacques was kind, funny, approachable. I realized survivors aren't just solemn black-and-white images in documentaries. They're alive. They're human. They still laugh. They still live.

And I realized—we always ask them about the war, the camps, the numbers, the trauma. But no one asks about after. How they rebuilt. And that's where the real inspiration is. Not just that they survived—but that they went on to live with such courage, grace, and dignity. That's what I wanted young people to see.

Leslie: What makes this project unique?

Sophie: I knew there were already large collections of Holocaust testimonies, like the massive USC archive. But those are long and formal—great for historians, yet not really accessible to most people.

Back then, there was almost nothing easily available online or on social media. I wanted to change that—to create something short, deeply human, easy to engage with, and designed for today's audience—especially young people. A ten-minute video might catch their attention. Then maybe they'll watch another, and another... and before they know it, they've binged five episodes and really learned something.
It's accessible because I don't play the "professional". I dive in like a child would—curious, a bit naïve, disarming. I ask simply, without pressure. And the survivors open up. I realized early on-they're not afraid of hurting me, because I'm not family. In fact, they often hit me with the full weight of their truth. Instead of and that shows, the result stands out. It's a different tone—raw and unfiltered.

Above all, I wanted it to be truly independent—no networks, no filters. Just a free and honest way to reach people, anytime, anywhere.

Leslie: What's the urgency today?

Sophie: It's twofold. First, soon there will be no more survivors left—and they want to speak before it's too late. The second urgency is the present moment itself: the alarming rise in antisemitism around the world.

The urgency is real. I saw the warning signs early. And when I met the first survivors, I realized something was off about how we talk about memory—this whole "Devoir de Mémoire" ("Duty of remembrance") idea, I never believed in it, Memory isn't a duty—it's a living, human process. And if we frame it as a moral obligation, we lose young people. Also, I never thought repeating "Never Again" like a mantra would work if you don't truly understand what happened.

This isn't just about Jews or the past. It's a universal story. A warning. Survivors don't speak out for pity or to be seen as victims. They speak to alert humanity to what people are capable of. To show the patterns. To teach the signs.

One survivor, Henri, told me: "History always repeats itself—but never exactly the same way. The danger is in the small differences."

They're not waiting for Nazis to march through Paris again. They see how hate mutates, and how antisemitism rises in cycles. They've lived it. They know silence and passivity are just as dangerous as action.

Lucette told me that when, in 2014 she heard chants of "Death to the Jews" from her window, What broke her wasn't just the words—it was how no one reacted. Just like in the '40s. People watched. People let it happen. That's what this project is about—breaking that silence.

For me, this project has always been about saying: you don't have to be a bystander. You can choose differently. You can act. Survivors rebuilt their lives from nothing—no family, no money—and they kept going. That's the message I want to pass on to my children. These are the heroes I want to show them.
It's not about changing the world. It's about showing we're still here. Alive. Standing. And reminding others not to look away when hate shows up—no matter where it comes from.

Sophie: For you that' a different story, you're a descendant of four Holocaust survivors. You were raised with that past in your bottle. What was it like growing up with that all around you?

Leslie: I don't even know if it was in the bottle—I think it was just in my veins. It was everywhere, in the air we breathed, in the way we grew up. It wasn't something anyone had to explain to me, like, "Sit down, I need to tell you something." No one ever did that. But we just knew. My twin brother and I always knew our grandparents were Holocaust survivors.

It wasn't a big revelation; it was just part of life. Papi and Mamie had been in the ghetto in Lodz, they came from Poland, and Tata Hanniah had been in the camps. Then there were Papated and Maminou—they were also from Poland, but for them, it was the Lwów ghetto, and then they were hidden in the forest.

And their friends?
Same story. Every single one of them was a survivor.

Even though my grandparents never talked about the Holocaust, it wasn't just silence—it was forbidden. Asking questions would get you in trouble. I would get the look, and I knew. I learned pretty quickly that this was something you just didn't bring up.
I remember trying one day with my grandmother.
She had just lit her candles before the holiday. She turned her hands three times toward her face, then covered her eyes to pray... and that's when I saw her crying—for the first time. So I asked, "Mamie, why are you crying?"

"Because I'm saying a prayer for my parents."
So I asked again, What happened to your parents?

"You're too curious. Curiosity is a bad habit. And I don't want to answer that question. You should never ask me something like that again."

That was it. Every time I tried to bring it up, I got the same kind of response. I could see how much pain it caused, so I stopped pushing.

Even though my grandparents never spoke about the Holocaust with us, that was only during the day. When I'd sleep slept over on weekends, I would hear them scream in their sleep. Nighttime was far more informative than the daytime. Silent by day, haunted by night.

I grew up with that silence.
A silence that took up so much space.

Sophie: To what extent is this history part of you? What impact did it have on you?

Leslie: You know, the first time I went to therapy, I was only five years old. And in France, in the '80s, that was really not common. Therapy wasn't something kids did. But I had so much anxiety—about sleep, about the dark, about food. I had food-related phobias—a deep fear of running out of food, but also a fear of vomiting or not being able to keep food down. To this day, I feel embarrassed even talking about it, but it completely consumed me.

My grandparents had been so deeply traumatized by starvation that it became part of my DNA. They starved. I didn't. All four of them went without food for years. The hunger stopped with them—but the trauma didn't. I carry it.

The Holocaust, it's fully part of me, whether I want it to be or not. You step into my house today, and the first thing you'll notice? Books. Everywhere. They pile up on shelves, spill onto my nightstand, take over the floor, even make their way into my bedroom. My husband—he's like you, this isn't his story—he's this close to losing it. But I can't stop. I need the books around me. And it's not just books—it's art, too. Even the art I buy, I realize, is almost always connected to that era. It's subconscious, but there it is, again and again.

There's no escaping it. Not that I even try.
This story, this history—it's in me, around me, shaping me, messing me up in ways I don't even fully understand.

Me too—I carry the weight of Auschwitz.

Facial Massage

Sophie: Is that why you decided to join The Last Ones? To start asking questions and finally break the silence?

Leslie: I had spent my whole life tiptoeing around that silence. I respected my grandparents too much to ask. I was terrified of hurting them. But after they were gone, the fear disappeared. There was no one left to protect from the truth—only a responsibility to uncover it. I've always been curious, almost painfully so. And once they were gone, I gave myself permission. That's when I started digging. That's when The Last Ones became a calling.

And then there's you, Sophie—chutzpah in one hand, cheesecake in the other, breaking every unspoken rule, crossing lines I never dared to touch. You got them to speak—all these survivors. You made them tell their stories: the ones from the camps, the ghettos, the forests, the hiding places... those who lived through starvation, disease, fear, grief, and total dehumanization.

And I thought, Damn. She had guts.
You didn't just open a door—you blew it wide open.
You gave me permission. You made me ask myself: What am I waiting for?

And together, we took The Last Ones global.
Now here we are, over three years later.
This project... It hits different. It matters.

I'm proud of us.

Sophie:

"One of the very first survivors I met, Elie Buzyn, said to me as we parted: 'You will become the witness of the witness that I am, it's a very important job.' From that moment on, my destiny — and Leslie's — was sealed."

Leslie and Sophie visiting Birkenau as part of The Last Ones project.

THE WITNESSES

Henri Borlant .66

Élie Buzyn .104

Frania Eisenbach .106

Hedy Fladell .124

Lucette Gejzenblozen .126

Ginette Kolinka .130

Ginette Krausz .164

Yvette Levy .166

Léon Lewkowicz .166

Nicolas Roth .212

Esther Senot .230

Judith Sherman .252

Jeanette Spiegel .256

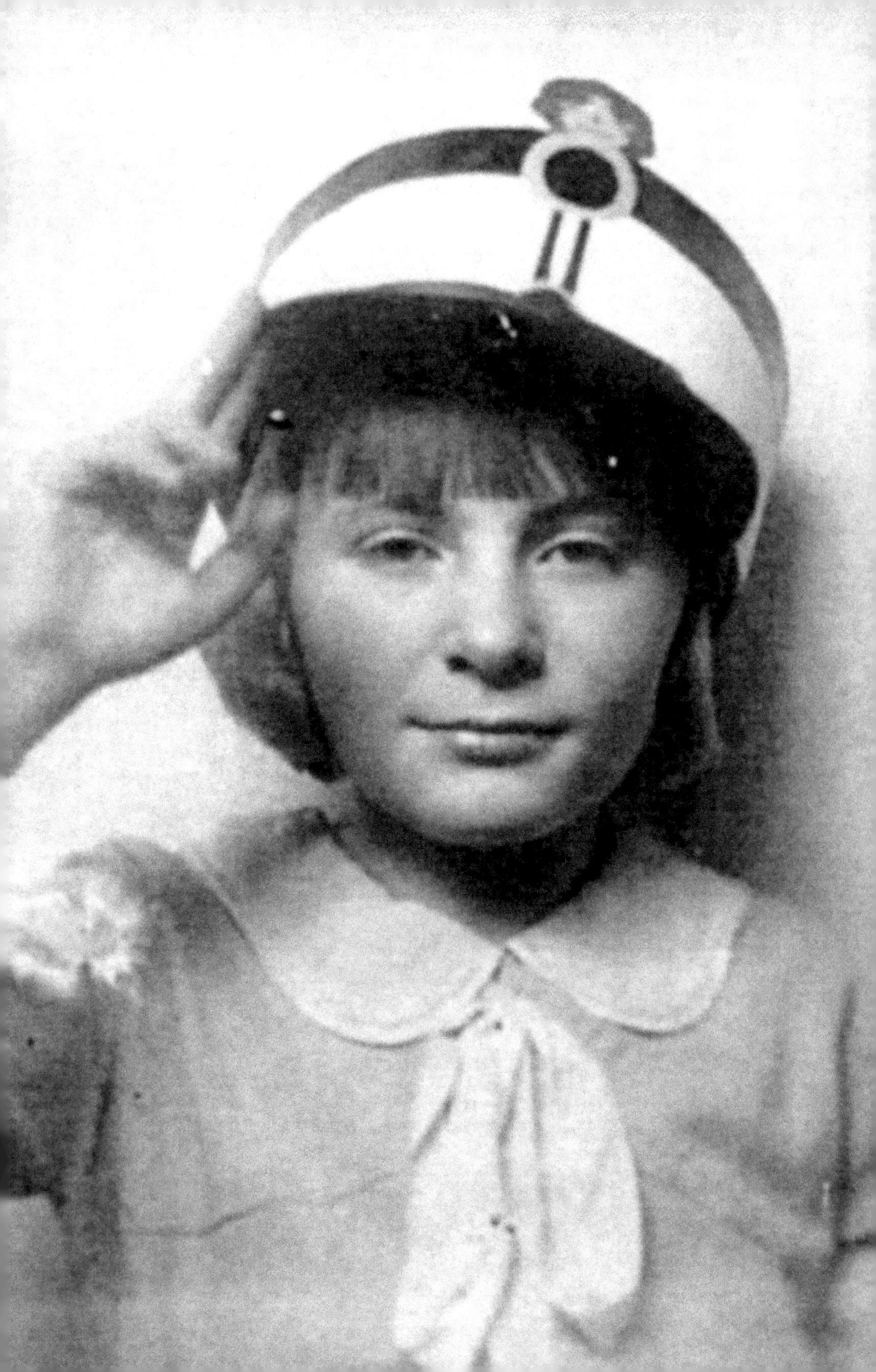

(1)

THE END OF INNOCENCE

Léon

I started suffering at nine. In Poland, even before the war, antisemitism ran deep. I was an only child. My mother had me late—around 45. I was a miracle, the center of her world. We were incredibly close. When it was time, she enrolled me in school and walked me there herself. We said goodbye with tears in our eyes. The bell rang for recess. We stepped out of the classroom, and that's when a group of Polish boys attacked me. They grabbed my arm, my neck, pushed me against a wall.

They threw me to the ground, and pulled down my pants to check if I was circumcised.

When they saw I was Jewish, they spat on me. That was my first humiliation—at such a young age. When I got home, my mother saw it on my face. I told her what happened. She sat down, pulled me onto her lap, and we cried together.

Then she said, "You're not going back."
And she meant it.
From that day on, she became my teacher.

Léon holding the portrait of his mother, whom he saw for the last time on the Birkenau ramp.

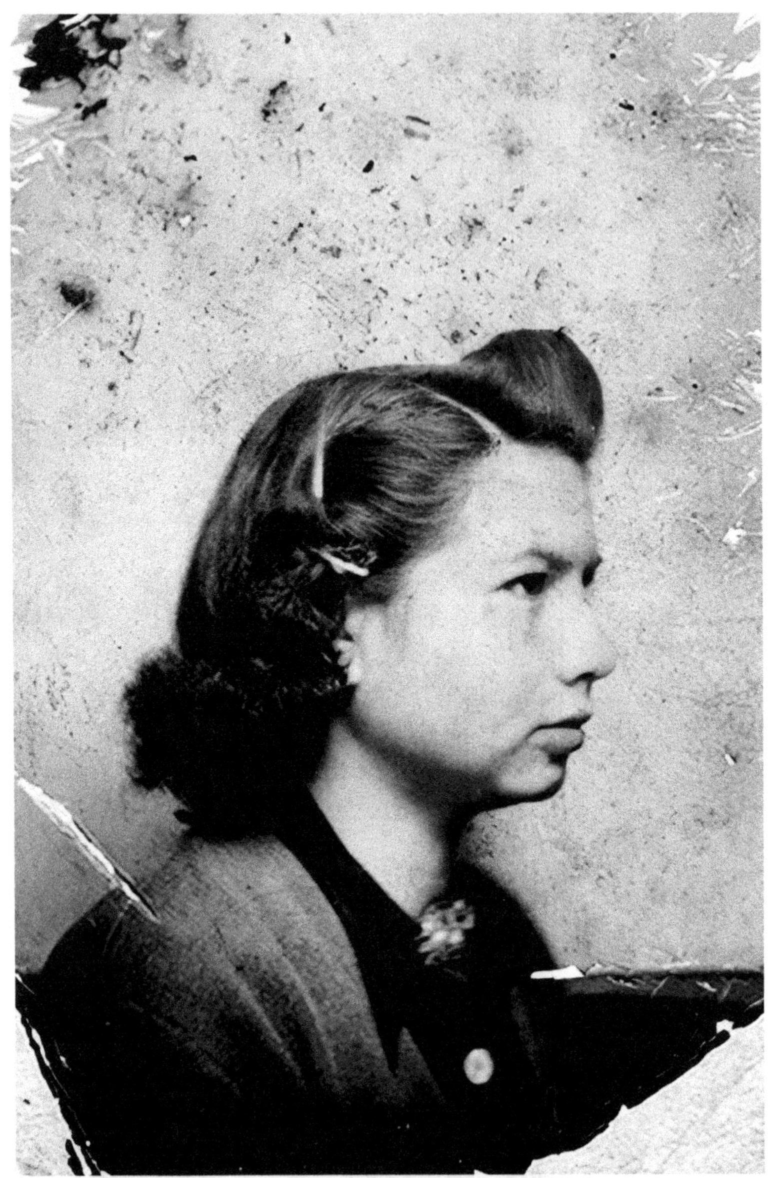

Esther Senot

Esther

In 1939, I was 11 years old. At the time, there were 300,000 Jews living in France. We didn't make up a very large proportion of the French population, but we were subjected to new laws that were extremely repressive. First of all, we had to go to the police station to be registered as Jews. We had to state where we lived, how many people were in our household, and give an inventory of what we owned. If we owned a bicycle or a radio, for example, we had to take it to the police station.

The police would then stamp our identification cards with the word "Juif" (jew) in red ink.

All professions were off limits to us: Jewish doctors, surgeons, dentists, journalists and lawyers were not allowed to practice. We were not allowed in public spaces. At the entrance of public parks, new signs were placed: "No Jews or dogs allowed." We were not allowed on the main avenues of Paris, such as the Champs-Élysées, or the Grands Boulevards. In public transportation, we were allowed only in the last row or car. The curfew forbade us to go out after 8:00 pm, and we were allowed in food stores only after 4:00 pm, when there was barely anything left. Life started to become very difficult at that time.

In working-class neighborhoods,
we lived one day at a time.

We got by like this until May 1941, when two of my brothers were summoned by the police for "family matters." My parents had taught us to be very respectful of the law and to trust the French police, so they went. They were immediately arrested. It was one of the first large roundups of men between the ages of 16 and 50. That day, 4,000 people were arrested and immediately sent to two French camps in the Loiret, established and overseen by the French: Pithiviers and Beaune-la-Rolande. I was 14 years old; I remember that my sister and I used to take care packages to my brothers, bribing the gendarmes, who were French armed officers.

Then, in June 1942, it became mandatory for Jews 6 years and older to wear the yellow star of David. We went to pick the yellow stars at the police station and we sewed them onto our clothing.

Sign at the entrance to a park which reads:
PLAYGROUND
RESERVED FOR CHILDREN
FORBIDDEN TO JEWS

Sarah Kanovitch and her three children sitting outside a public garden during the occupation of Paris — only the two boys would survive.

"We were not allowed in public spaces. At the entrance of public parks, there was a sign: 'No Jews or dogs allowed.'"

- ESTHER -

Hedy

Until I was 12, life was just as I had always known it. I lived with my family in a small town in Romania. I remember the first time we heard about antisemitism—some Jewish men had been attacked and robbed. And then, I saw it with my own eyes. People were smashing the windows of Jewish stores, breaking everything, looting whatever they could. Glass everywhere. Shattered storefronts. My mother called the police. But the Hungarian police! They were worse than the Nazis.

Not long after that, we were made to wear the yellow star. The yellow star on our clothes. They announced that anyone caught without it would be severely punished. And then came the curfew. Six o'clock. Any Jew found on the streets after six would suffer the consequences.

But that wasn't enough for them. After that, they formed a ghetto. Actually, several ghettos across the city. They gathered all the Jewish people—everyone from the city, and the neighboring towns—and they forced us inside. It was overcrowded, the conditions were unsanitary, and we were constantly persecuted. One of the ghettos started right on my street. They boarded up our windows and doors.

We couldn't even step outside.
We were trapped.

Hedy holding a photo of her and her family, she is the only one who survived.

Yellow Star A yellow six-pointed Star of David badge that Jews were forced to wear on their clothing in Nazi-occupied Europe to mark and segregate them. The word "Jew" was often printed in the center. The badge became a symbol of humiliation, persecution, and resistance.

Henri

At the end of August 1939, I was twelve years old, living in Paris, in the 13th district. The war had not yet started but there were alarming rumors. The French authorities had decided to force people in the working-class neighborhoods. Those who had a lot of children had to move to various towns in the French countryside, depending on where they lived. Our family was sent to Angers. My mother, my sisters, and I left in a hurry, taking almost nothing with us. My mother was 9 months pregnant. On September 1st, she gave birth to my little sister Raymonde. My father, who had stayed in Paris for work and my 14-year-old brother Bernard later came to meet us.

We settled in a village, 15 miles from Angers. Despite the occupation, we went to school. It was a Catholic school. My brother and I were the best students in the class, including religious instruction. We discovered catechism and sacred history; these subjects were given twice the weight of the other classes. The priest who taught us liked us very much, and I admired him a lot. When he asked my parents if I could get baptized, my father said yes. He must have thought that when the war was over, we would go back home and forget all about it. So, I was baptized. I took my Holy Communion and became a churchgoer. I saw this teacher as someone extraordinary and thought that when I grew up, I would be just like him.

Sophie: What do you mean, just like him? A priest?

Henri: Yes, I admired him a lot. I was a 13- or 14-year-old kid, and I wanted to enter the seminary. I had my little baptism and confirmation medals.

Sophie: So, then you were deported as a Jew, when in your head, you were Catholic?

Henri: You got it!

Henri's sisters.

Nicolas to the left of his father, mother, brothers and sisters.

"My parents were exemplary citizens, they respected the law, including all the decrees, to the letter. Everything had to go through the official channels, they brought us up that way, so we obeyed."

- NICOLAS -

Nicolas

The Nazis arrived late, March 19, 1944, in Hungary, Germany's ally. Everything changed overnight. When refugees used to tell my parents stories about what was going on in other countries in Europe, my parents would reply, 'This can't be happening here!' They were convinced of it. After all, they were born in the 19th century, during la Belle Époque, a period of peace and prosperity.

They loved their country
and thought that it would all be over one day.

Suddenly, anti-Jewish laws were passed. We had to give up everything we owned: our cars, our radio sets, etc. Our bank accounts had to be declared, and our newspapers were banned. Every day, a new decree applying only to Jews was passed.

Saul

It was five in the morning. I was at home in bed in Tarpa, Hungary, when there was a knock on our window. We were ordered to report to the schoolyard by ten o'clock, carrying no more than fifteen pounds of personal belongings. Failure to show meant the gendarmes would come for you.

I was just a boy,
but that morning felt like the end of my childhood.

They forced us into horse-drawn wagons and transported us to a larger town, where they created a ghetto. Soon, it overflowed, so they moved us to a brick factory, just a roof held up by pillars with no walls. We tried to hang sheets for privacy, but with 50 to 70 families crammed into the same space, privacy was nothing more than a memory.

There was barely enough food to keep us alive. After three weeks, they stripped us of our remaining valuables and marched us to a train station.

Saul's father.

Irene

It was 1939, and Poland had already been invaded. The rise in antisemitism was harsh and swift. I went to school every day with my two best friends. One day, I waited for them, but they had gone to school without me. When I arrived, a Ukrainian teacher had already replaced ours. She used a big stick to single out all the Jewish students. She told us to leave and never come back.

That was the day I was thrown out of school for being Jewish. No one wanted to be my friend, or even talk to me. My two best friends called me a "Christ killer". I was only eleven years old; I went home crying.

From one day to the next,
I had no friends and I was afraid to leave the house.

Irene.

KOPP & JOSEPH
Deutsche!
Wehrt Euch!
Kauft nicht bei Juden!
Jude

“No one wanted to be my friend or even talk to me. My two best friends called me a ‘Christ killer’. I was only eleven years old.”

- IRENE -

Little Leon on the left with his family.

Leon

Anti-Semitism was everywhere in Poland way before the war broke out. It was a way of life. I heard the hateful words “dirty Jew”. Jews had to follow strict rules, like wearing the yellow star, but I refused. I never wore that star, never obeyed the travel restriction. Maybe it was my way of rebelling.

In 1942, they wiped out the entire Jewish community in my town. It was a quiet day in April when I saw the execution take place. About ten people were lined up and shot one by one, their bodies falling to the ground. I was barely 16 years old. I stood there, watching, unable to move.

What I saw that day is something
no one should ever have to witness.

By August 20 of that year, nearly every Jew in our town and the surrounding areas had been deported. Families were torn apart, homes abandoned, and life as I knew it vanished. I was supposed to be among them, but by some twist of fate, I wasn’t. Instead, I was working near a bridge while my family and friends were taken away. After that, the town was empty.

The silence was haunting.

Nissen

It was seven o'clock in the morning, Friday morning. My mother had gone out to buy groceries, preparing for Shabbat dinner. My sister and I had stayed home with our father. It was a typical day for us until they knocked on the door. Seven Gestapo; you know, the secret police of the Nazis. They Marched into our apartment. They asked who lived there. My father answered it was only him and the two kids.

Then one of the SS men asked about my mother. My father said she was at the marketplace. The chief Gestapo turned to my sister ordered her to get dressed. Go find your mother and bring her home immediately.

I didn't want her to go alone, so I asked to go as well.
And we went.

Halfway to the market, we saw our mother. She was carrying two heavy baskets—chicken, fish, cake, fruits, everything for Shabbat. We ran to her. Mama! Seven SS and the Gestapo are at the house!

Her hands started shaking. She knew exactly what that meant. She didn't even hesitate. Let's run home. If Papa is taken to Auschwitz, I want to go with him. Can you imagine! She didn't even think about saving us, her own children. My sister knew we had to save ourselves. She grabbed my arm and whispered, Now is not the time to speak. Run!

We ran...
I wasn't sure I'd ever see my mother again.
I could barely breathe.

Judith

Life was as you would expect for me, until around the age of nine. That's when things changed. Hitler rose to power, and suddenly Jewish children were no longer welcome in public schools in Slovakia. We were accused of poisoning the air by simply breathing. They believed our presence polluted the environment for the other children.

One night, something happened that changed everything for me. German soldiers barged into our house, armed with rifles—those old ones with bayonets, the knives fixed to the tips. I'll never forget the feeling of that bayonet pressing against my head. I was only nine. They were looking for "the man with the beard"—my father. All of us, my aunts, uncles, and cousins, were lined up against a wall, in our pajamas with rifles pointed at us. My mother, in her typical bravery, stood up to them. "Either shoot us or leave us alone!" My stomach sank. Would they really shoot us right there? Thankfully, they left, but only because it wasn't yet time for them to kill Jews.

This was when we were forced to wear yellow stars, marking us as Jews. In our village, it wasn't even necessary—everyone already knew who we were. But everything changed. Our friends changed. Our neighbors changed. We were no longer just the Jewish family in the village. We had become the enemy.

Judith with her mother, father, brother and sister.

REPARATUR
ahrrad Reparatur Werkstätte
Alois Aigner
43
SCHUH-HAUS
LEO SCHLESINGER

“I saw it with my own eyes. People were smashing the windows of Jewish stores, breaking everything, looting whatever they could. Glass everywhere.”

- HEDY -

The Night of Broken Glass

A state-sponsored pogrom that took place on November 9–10, 1938. Synagogues were burned, Jewish businesses were destroyed, and thousands of Jews were arrested across Nazi Germany and Austria.

Jacques Altmann

Jacques, whose birth name was Adolphe, was born in 1923. He grew up in Romainville with his three brothers, soon joined by an orphaned cousin whom they considered to be their fifth sibling.

The day the police came to his house, Jacques wasn't there. His parents and brothers were arrested. Eventually, he will be arrested, but he managed to escape from the police headquarters. Arrested a second time, he was made to stripped naked in the street. He was then sent to Drancy and then to Lévitan, a Parisian furniture store requisitioned to sort looted Jewish goods. It was there that he saw the who's who in Paris come to shop for free.

Deported to Birkenau on convoy 68, he was selected to work in a special kommando, named "Kanada", which, among other things, acted as a "welcoming committee". This group of deportees, in a slightly less dilapidated state than the others, was stationed on the ramp when the trains arrived - a staged operation designed to reassure the new arrivals and keep them compliant. Afterwards, the kommando's task was to empty the cars and to sort out the belongings left behind; the valuables would be sent to Germany, and worn or damaged clothing given to deportees.

Jacques saw hundreds of thousands of people pass through the gates, most of them going straight to their deaths. Among them, were his beloved grandparents. He saw them, and his friends had to hold him down so he wouldn't follow his grandparents to their death. After the war, he returned to Romainville but Adolphe would find not one family member.

He changed his first name to "Jacques", in memory of one of his murdered younger brothers. Jacques was the first former deportee I ever met and therefore the inspiration for Les Derniers/The Last Ones project.

Saul Blau

Saul Blau was born in 1930 in Tarpa, Hungary, the sixth of seven children in an observant Jewish family. At thirteen, he and his family were torn from their home and deported to Auschwitz, where his parents and younger sister were murdered. On arrival, a block elder pointed to the crematorium chimney and told him his parents had already been gassed and cremated; from that moment, he understood his only task was survival.

Selected for labor, Saul was sent to a coal-mine camp in the Auschwitz industrial complex and endured months of starvation, sickness, and fear. In January 1945 he was driven on a death march to Buchenwald, where U.S. forces liberated him later that year.

After the war, he returned to Hungary to search for surviving relatives before immigrating to Israel. In the new Jewish homeland, he joined the fledgling Israeli Air Force, beginning to rebuild a life from the ashes of his childhood.

Saul remained in Israel for seven years before moving to the United States to reunite with his siblings. There, he met Viola, and together they built a new life — and a family — raising two sons, Robert and Andrew.

Even today, Saul carries a spark of youth, as if determined to live fully the life that was almost taken from him. Handsome behind the wheel of his car, he radiates an energy that feels both defiant and alive — a man who refuses to let time, or history, slow him down.

Henri Borlant

Henri was born in Paris in 1927, into a large and very modest Russian family. Years earlier, his paternal and maternal grandparents had fled the pogroms raging in Tsarist Russia, where Jews were victims of rape and murder.

They arrived in France penniless and without speaking a word of French. At the end of August 1939, when Henri was twelve, the authorities decided to evacuate children from working-class neighborhoods to the French countryside. The family ended up in a village near Angers, where the children attended a Catholic school.

Henri was top of his class, including in catechism instruction. He was then baptized and received holy Communion. He admired the priest so much that he considered becoming a priest himself. A few months later, in July 1942, Henri, who felt he more Catholic than Jewish, was deported to Auschwitz, along with his father, his sister Denise and his brother Bernard, who would die very quickly.

Henri spent more than two years there, learning all the languages of the camp and eventually being considered an "elder", which earned him the respect of the other prisoners. He was then transferred to Sachsenhausen and Ohdruf, a subcamp of Buchenwald, from which he managed to escape. Without realizing it, he played a historic role by alerting American soldiers who were in a nearby village of the existence of the camps. They then saw for themselves the appalling reality.

Upon his return to Paris, he was fortunate enough to find his mother, who had managed to hide with her other children, enabling him to resume his life and to study medicine. He married Hella, a German woman and together they have four daughters.

After years of silence, the need to speak became more pressing, but it wasn't until the 1990s that he felt he was ready to talk about his past.

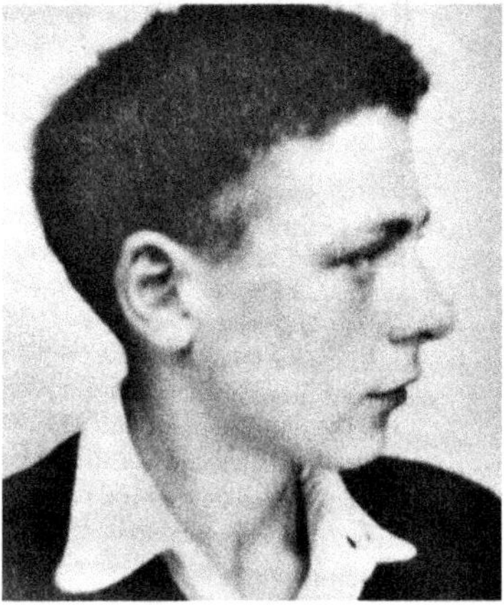

(2)

THE ARREST

Judith

Our lives were in danger, so my parents sent my sister and me to live with a non-Jewish family in Prešov. It was the only way to keep us safe. We lived in constant fear, hiding in the shadows, never turning on lights at night, and never speaking of our presence to anyone. Every sound made us jump. Every knock on the door felt like it might be the end.

But even with all these precautions, we were betrayed. The Gestapo came for us, arriving with a truck full of soldiers. The noise they made as they arrested us was deafening, as if they wanted the entire neighborhood to know what happens to those who hide Jews. It wasn't just about taking us.

They weren't just capturing us, they were sending a message to everyone. Anyone who hid Jews did so at the risk of their lives.

I managed to escape and hid in the forest with a group of other Jews, including my aunt. We moved constantly, always looking over our shoulders. I was only twelve years old, living in constant fear of being discovered. One morning, I woke up to the sharp point of a bayonet, yet again, pressing against my head. German soldiers had found us again. They forced us out of hiding, not allowing us to take anything with us. I remember the woman next to me asking, "Can I take my coat?". The soldier struck her. We weren't allowed to take anything.

Judith holding a photo of her family — all of whom perished in the camps.

David

In 1940, my father was arrested at our home in Czechoslovakia and sent to a labor camp. I didn't understand why—he had done nothing wrong. One day he was there, the next, gone. No explanation. No goodbye.

A year later, when I was 13, they came for the rest of us.

It was the Hlinka Guards—the Slovak Nazi party. But these weren't faceless soldiers from far away. These men were no strangers. They were our neighbors. People we greeted in the streets, people we had shared meals with, people we trusted. Now, they wore uniforms and acted as collaborators with the Nazis. And they were the ones who came to tear our family apart.

They stormed into our home with sticks and guns. They shouted orders, beat us, and forced us out. We were given just ten minutes—ten minutes to gather a lifetime. I remember grabbing my schoolbag and one of my father's books. That's all I could think to take. My hands were shaking. My mother was crying. My siblings stood frozen. We didn't know where we were going—only that we had to go.

And then, just like that,
one of the guards shouted: "No more minutes!"

Nissen

Early one morning in our home in Bratislava, we heard a noise upstairs—a sudden commotion.

Someone shouted, "Look out!" SS officers had come. They searched through the entire house, turning everything upside down. Then one of them started climbing up to the attic.

He began pulling away the stacks of hay, one by one. They were thorough. They knew how to search. I held my breath. If they pulled away too much, they would find us. More and more hay disappeared. I thought to myself, "They'll see us, they'll see us!" I prayed that the last bit of hay would be enough to hide us.

I was just ten years old. My childhood ended that morning—when our hiding place was discovered. The soldiers ordered us to get dressed. And then they took us.

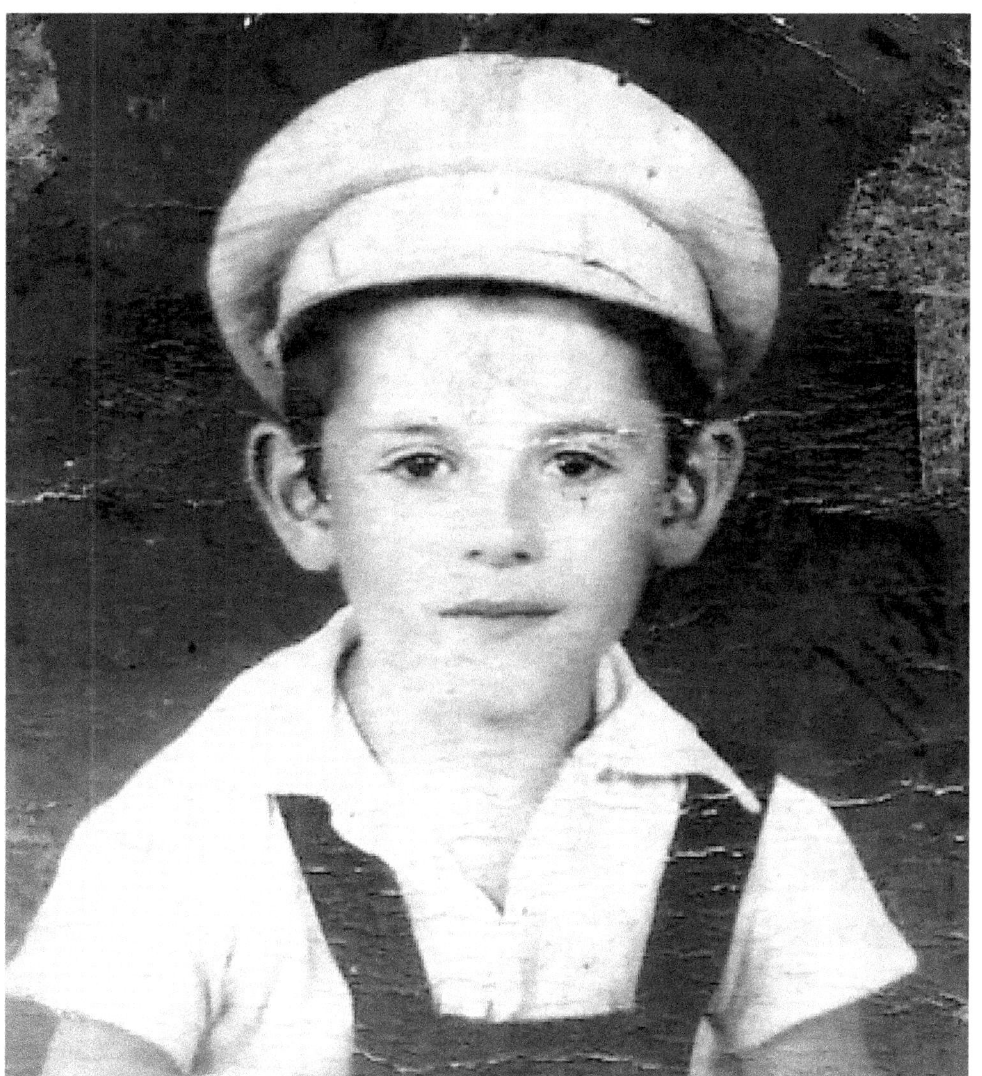

Nissen.

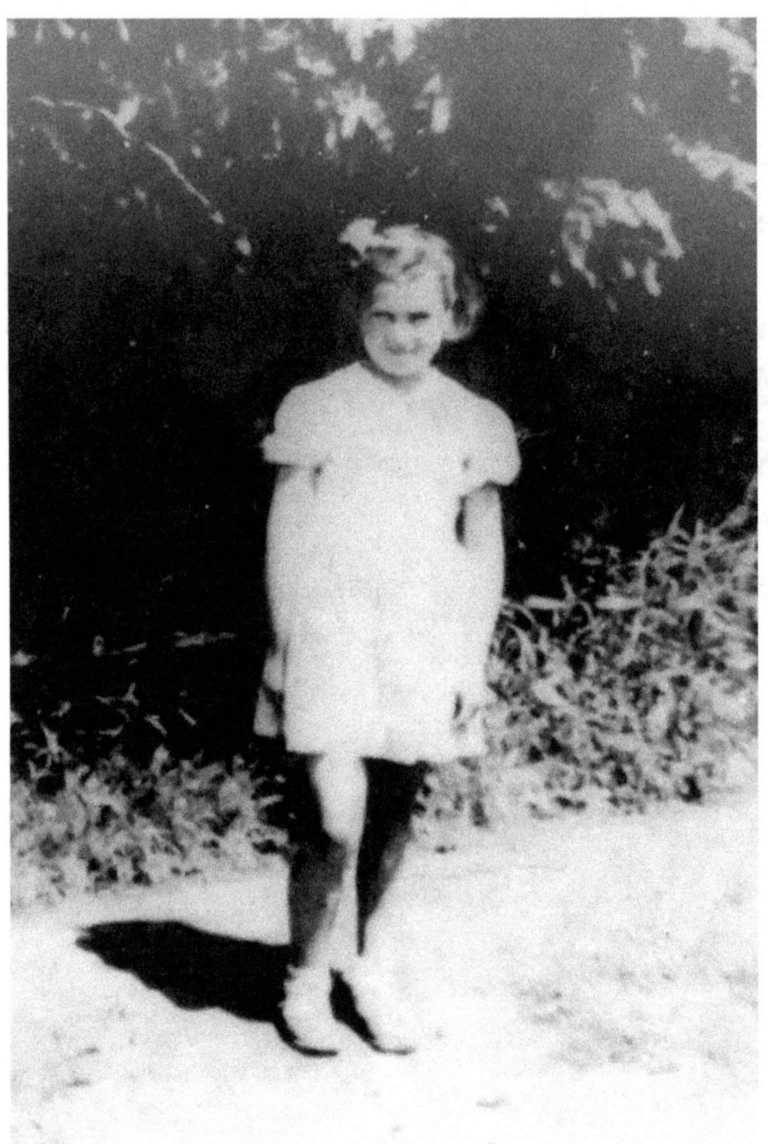

Irene.

Irene

We lived in a small Carpathian town. Life was ordinary—until the Nazis came.

They ordered us to pack, no more than 24 kilos. There was no refusing, no running, no hiding. They had already gone through the town records, marking every Jewish family. Soldiers and local collaborators had names, addresses, and instructions. They knew exactly where to find us.

Before we left the house, my mother picked out a skirt for me. It was blue, with little flowers on it. A small gesture of comfort in a moment of fear. Then, she handed me four diamonds and whispered, "If we get separated and you're hungry, use these to buy bread." I didn't fully understand, but I could tell from her eyes that she was scared in a way I had never seen before.

They marched us from our homes, down the street to the railroad station. Neighbors stood outside, some watching silently, others joining in the cruelty. As we walked, our so-called "friends" were yelling, "Get out of here, Jews! We don't need you here!" and "It's about time they take you away!" Their words cut deeper than any weapon. These were people we had once trusted—now shouting with hatred.

At one point, I heard a baby crying. I stepped out of line to find the baby, to help. My instincts took over. That's when a man took his rifle and pushed me back towards the line. That man was my father's best friend! He had laughed with us at Shabbat dinners. And now, he was threatening me "Do that again, I will shoot you". My heart was pounding, the world was spinning. I froze. My father pulled me close. I was told that from now on, I do as I'm told and nothing else.

Sarah

I am an only child. The day of the Vel' d'Hiv' roundup, I was at home with my mother. The French police came to get us and put us on a crowded bus. We drove through Paris towards the Velodrome d'Hiver. Once there, my mother tried to find out what was going to happen to us. She was told that we were going to be sent to Germany to work. My mother told me that I would probably go to school there and that we would meet at the end of the day. As the day went by, the Velodrome d'Hiver filled up. At the time, of course, we didn't know that this roundup would be the biggest one in France during World War II. More than 13,000 people were arrested on July 16 and 17, a third of whom were children who were confined there then sent to Auschwitz.

Only about a hundred people came back.

Around 5:00 pm, we saw paraplegics and amputees in wheelchairs, and even dying people on stretchers. It was obvious that these people were going to die. My mother told me: "They lied to us; these people can't be sent to work. Something much worse is afoot." That's when she decided to escape. She sent me off first and told me to meet her at the house of some non-Jewish friends on the other side of Paris. Miraculously, we found each other at a subway stop close to the friends' house. They hid us for several weeks, then we went from hiding place to hiding place for two years. Despite that, I managed to still go to school.

But one morning, at 7:00 am, fifteen minutes before I was supposed to leave for school, two young police inspectors in civilian clothes came to arrest us. We had been reported to the police. I'll never forget, I had my report card in my hand and I showed it to them. They told me: "You are a good student, what do you want to do when you grow up?" I answered, "I want to be a doctor." They told me, "Where we are sending you, you will be able to continue!" Still today, I wonder if they were being naïve or cynical.

This time, we were not able to escape,
and the next day we were on the list for Drancy.

Sarah and her parents.

Vel' d'Hiv' An indoor sports stadium in Paris, used during the mass roundup of Jews in July 1942. Over 13,000 Jews, including more than 4,000 children, were held there, under inhumane conditions, before being sent to Drancy and then deported. Most of them were gassed in Auschwitz.

Esther

On July 16th, 1942, in Belleville, the neighborhood where I used to live, a rumor of an impending roundup began to spread. I was 14 years old and home for summer break.

Until then, the roundups were only for men; woman and children had not been arrested yet. So, men were the only ones in hiding. Only women, children and elderly people were in the apartments. The infamous Vel' d'Hiv' roundup was starting.

We heard noises, including baton blows on the doors. Because of the census, the police knew exactly where to go. They told people to prepare little travel bags and to give their pets to the building attendants. They broke down the doors of those who refused to open. I saw elderly people taken downstairs on stretchers and women with babies jumping out of the windows so they wouldn't be arrested. It was awful. Oddly enough, nobody came to our place, A little bit later in the day, when things seemed to have quieted down, my mom, worried sick, asked me and one of my sisters to go outside to see what was going on. We went in opposite directions. When I came back an hour later, our apartment was empty: my father, mother, brothers and sisters had all disappeared, and there were seals on the door. I was left all alone, just like that, wearing only a little summer dress.

I had never left my neighborhood or my parents.

After several hours, not knowing what to do, I went to my brother and sister-in-law's apartment to see if there was anybody left. There, the building attendant told me, "It's no use going upstairs. Nobody's there." I started crying and told her I didn't know where to go. So, she agreed to hide me. I stayed with her for two weeks. It was an enormous risk for her. Then, I went to Pau to rejoin the last brother I had left. He kept me hidden in a maid's room for three months.

Then, naively, I went back to Paris to see if my parents had come back. Obviously, that wasn't the case.

I was arrested in the middle of Paris during an identification check. I was 15 years old and didn't have the proper identification, so the police took me to the station behind city hall. A few days later, I was in Drancy. I was deported on September 2nd, 1943, as part of convoy 59.

Julia

My mother was arrested during the Vel' d'Hiv' roundup. A few months later, the French police knocked at our door. I was with my father, who wasn't French. I am French, so I thought I would be safe. My father hid in a closet, and I opened the door to the police. But when he heard them handcuffing me, he came out of his hiding place. He didn't want to leave me by myself; I was crying, asking him why he hadn't stayed hidden.

We learned later that the neighbors from the 2nd floor had reported us. The police didn't hesitate to tell us that before taking us away.

“My father was hiding there, in this apartment where I still live today.”

- JULIA -

Lucette

My story is a little complicated; my life has not been simple. I was arrested in Lyon with my parents just after we celebrated my 20th birthday. The day after my birthday, I heard someone running in the stairway. I opened the door, and I saw a man wearing civilian clothing holding a gun. My first thought was that he must be a thief. I didn't know people could be arrested just like that. He came into our apartment, opened the window and whistled. In the building across from ours, a woman opened a window to see what was going on. He shouted at her, "Close your window or I'll put a bullet in your head." She closed the window, then he shot a bullet into the ceiling.

Then, a whole regiment came up.

We were taken to the militia's office, where they asked my father to give them names of his comrades. He replied, "I don't have any. You've already arrested everyone." They hit him in the face. I thought my mother was going to faint, so I planted myself in front of the guy who was beating up my father and I told him, "Today you hit my father, but when the allies land, it will be your turn." I was a shy young girl, but I couldn't stand seeing my father being beaten. It was too much for me. Another prisoner came and stood beside me and said that I was right. So, the militia man took out his gun and threatened to shoot us both. I didn't say anything more. I understood, that moron was capable of carrying out his threats.

After that, we were taken to the Gestapo, which was headed by Klaus Barbie. There, I saw two men attached to each other, one of whom was being beaten up. The floor was covered with blood. I was against the wall with my mother. The man fell, almost at my feet. The blood spurted from his open skull, and the man to whom he was attached fell on top of him. I screamed.

You can't imagine the horror.

Lucette's parents

> "I was a shy young girl,
> but I couldn't stand seeing my father
> being beaten."
>
> **- LUCETTE -**

klaus Barbie was a German officer of the Schutzstaffel and Sicherheitsdienst who worked in Vichy France during World War II. He became known as the "Butcher of Lyon" for having personally tortured prisoners—primarily Jews and members of the French Resistance—as the head of the Gestapo in Lyon.

TORLEY

Jacques

I wasn't home the day my family was arrested; I was in Nantes, with a resistance network. My mother, father, and four brothers, who were still very young, were taken to Drancy, where they left for Auschwitz via convoy 40. They were all gassed upon their arrival before they even entered the camp, as was the case for all children under 16.

A few months later, it was my turn to be arrested by the Gestapo. I had a fake ID, but they wanted to be sure, so they told me: "Take your pants down." I refused. I was much too ashamed. We were not used to seeing each other naked or showing our genitals. So, they stripped me down in the middle of the street, in front of everyone, including my friends. I could no longer deny that I was Jewish. They took me to Drancy then to Auschwitz-Birkenau.

"They stripped me down in the middle of the street, in front of everyone. I could no longer deny that I was Jewish."

- JACQUES -

Jacques on his father's left, with his mother and brothers.
No one came back except him.

Henri's parents.

Henri

On August 15, 1942, after living three years in a village next to Angers, we were arrested. The police had a list, and they arrested all the Jews aged 15 to 50. I had just turned 15 on June 5. My brother Bernard was 17, my sister Denise 21, and my mother 42. My father was 54, so they left him behind with the youngest kids.

We didn't know where they were taking us; we they were sending us to work somewhere.

My mother struggled. After multiple pregnancies, she had put on considerable extra weight and couldn't walk more than 300 hundred feet. I was terrified that my mother, whom I adored, would be taken away. We were taken to the big seminary in Angers. After two days, without any explanation, they brought mommy back to the house and took daddy instead. Later I tried to find out why, but I never got an answer.

When we were about to leave in the cattle cars for Auschwitz, some of us threw notes for our families onto the tracks. There were almost always some railroad workers to pick up our "letters" and deliver them to the intended recipients. I get emotional when I talk about it, because in France, close to 76,000 Jews were deported, and 97% of them were killed. So, for them, these notes were their dying words.

When I came back, I was extremely lucky to find my mother. She had this note in her wallet.

Jeanette

It was April 1st, 1944—April Fool's Day. But there was no joke. The Gestapo came for me. I was fifteen years old, still hiding in Brussels, when my luck finally ran out.

They knocked on the door,
they knew exactly who they were looking for.

When they entered, they smiled. They spoke gently, almost kindly. "Oh, please pack everything you want, don't leave anything behind. Take a suitcase," they spoke so nicely, so we packed. We carefully folded clothes, placed small keepsakes inside, trying to hold on to what little we could.

And then, we left. But the suitcase didn't come with me. None of it did. Once we were out the door, the polite smiles faded, and our belongings stayed behind—in their hands, in their pockets, in their possession as if they had always been theirs.

There was a man with them, dressed in civilian clothes. He was Belgian. He was helping them. I looked at him and screamed, "Are you Belgian? Are you helping them?" My voice was shaking with rage. He didn't answer. Instead, one of the Gestapo officers struck me hard across the face. The sting spread through my cheek, but I refused to cry.

They took me to Rue de la Loi, the Gestapo headquarters in Brussels. I wasn't alone. My friend Sophie—her real name was Sara. We were thrown into a dark, damp cellar. The air was thick, and the walls seemed to close in around us. No food. No light. Just the sound of footsteps above, reminding us that we were trapped... and for good.

Leon

I was sent to prison for a few days. It was cold, dark, and terrifying. I remember hearing the cries of others through the walls—some begging, some screaming. I was so scared. I had no idea why I was there and what was going to happen to me.

From there, they sent me to the Tarnów ghetto.

It was a living hell. The conditions were unbearable. The daily struggle just to survive felt endless. We were crammed into a tiny space, with almost no food and even less hope. Disease spread quickly. People died every day. It was there that I truly understood how far their cruelty could go. Each day was a fight to survive. We had to be careful—any wrong move, any glance in the wrong direction, could lead to a beating, or worse. They made us feel like we were nothing, like our lives had no value. And somehow, I kept going.

Jews arrested by the Germans in the Tarnow ghetto, standing on trucks on their way to the Pustkow forced labor camp.

Deportation from Tarnow

Frania

Together with the rest of my family, we were locked up in the Tarnow ghetto, one of the first ghettos in Poland. There were constantly what they called “actions.” The order was given to close the shutters and windows so that people couldn’t see what was happening in the street, but the door had to stay open so the Germans could come in easily.

They would come in and shoot people on the spot.

One day, when things had quieted down, I went to visit a family I knew, the Blatt family. They were all lying on the ground, dead, and there was an 18-month-old baby lying in blood, screaming. I couldn’t bring myself to step over all those bodies to get to the baby. I ran away. I went back home and told my mother, who told me not to go out again. I don’t know what happened to that baby.

Later, they came back and selected people, including us. I remember my mother holding my hand, and we were being hit on the head with whips. Then, in the chaos—I don’t know if it was my mother who let go of my hand or if I let go of hers—but we were separated. I didn’t see her again, I never found her again, and that haunts me to this day. I can still feel the blows on our heads, my hand gripping hers tightly— and then nothing.

Never again.

Léon

They took everything from us.

My father was fired from his newspaper. They froze his bank account and took all his money. We were forced out of our apartment—we weren't allowed to take anything except one table. Just a plain kitchen table. Everything else had to stay behind: the silverware, the menorah, every trace of the life we had built.

We were sent to the ghetto. Lodz. I used to call it a "chalet"—it was just a wooden shack. I don't even know how many of us were crammed in there. Each family was given fifteen square meters to live in. We had to wear a yellow star—one on the chest, one on the back.

Then came the child hunts.
I was just a kid, hiding in a suitcase under a bed.
That's where I slept.

In the ghetto, there was nothing. No food. No medicine. People dragged themselves through the streets. There was poverty, desperation. And everything was eaten. Nothing went to waste. Everything was eaten. Anything. Everything. No matter what.

People were dying constantly. Every morning, I'd come downstairs and see bodies lined up in front of the buildings—those who had died during the night. Some were still clothed, but later in the day, they'd be stripped bare. People would take the clothes.

I wandered through it all.
I saw everything. Every day, the same images:
Death, death, death.

smetyka
UMOWE

Élie Buzyn

Élie was born in 1929 in the city of Lodz, which from April 1940 onwards was home to one of Poland's largest ghettos. He survived there with his parents and sister, until they were deported to Auschwitz in 1944. Élie was then 15 years old. His parents were immediately murdered and he lost track of his sister. When the camp was liquidated, he survived the death marches to Buchenwald, where, like Armand Bulwa, he was one of the nine hundred adolescents who survived.

After the war, Élie had nothing left. He stayed in France for a while, and managed to find his sister and one of his uncles in Paris, but he couldn't bear staying any longer on the stained soil of Europe. So, he left for Israel to build a new world.

After working on a kibbutz for eight years, he decided to return to France to study medicine, and he became an orthopedic surgeon. The fact that his feet froze in Buchenwald after the death march inspired him to study this specialty. He explains how hard it was for him to rebuild himself. To do so, he had to "put on blinders", to prevent him from looking back or even sideways. Thinking back about his past and what he went through would make him want to commit suicide.

He had three children with his wife Etty, but he never talked about his deportation with them. He considered that this would be like injecting them with his own pain "intravenously". They knew, but didn't talk about it. And then, time went by and eight grandchildren were born. Time and the birth of new generations made him see things differently. The grandchildren started asking questions.

One day, his son announced that he would like to go to Auschwitz to see the place where his grandparents were murdered. Élie decided to go with him. When his grandchildren each turned 15, he took them there. Fifteen is meaningful as it was the age Élie was when he was deported. His grandchildren represent an unbroken chain of generations, something the Nazis tried to destroy, but failed.

Frania Eisenbach

Frania Eisenbach was born on March 1, 1926, in Tarnów, a city in southern Poland. She came from a family of musicians: her father was a symphony conductor, and her mother played piano in the city's cinemas. She had two older brothers, one of whom was a violinist.

In September 1939, Tarnów was invaded by the Germans. When Frania's father learned he was being hunted by the occupiers, he decided to flee. In 1941, Frania and the rest of her family were confined to the Tarnów Ghetto. She recalls horrific scenes — including discovering an entire family of friends murdered in their home, except for a baby lying among the bodies.

In September 1943, during the liquidation of the ghetto, Frania was with her mother, but in the chaos she lost her hand and never saw her again. Frania was deported to the Plaszów camp, where she remained for eight months. In May 1944, she was sent to Auschwitz, where she was selected to repair clothing taken from murdered prisoners.

In November 1944, she was transferred to the Flossenbürg concentration camp, where she worked in a factory making machine parts, and later to Theresienstadt.

At the end of the war, she made her way to France, arriving in Paris on June 10, 1945.

Frania was the only survivor of a family of sixty. She told me, with deep emotion, that she still cries whenever she hears music — because it brings her back to her family and to the image of her mother's fingers on the piano keys.

Flora Eskenazi

Flora was born in Marseille in 1925 to a Greek father and a Turkish mother, both traveling ice-cream vendors. She grew up in a happy family of six children.

In 1939, the family left Marseille for the small town of Barjols, where Flora lived until her father's arrest. He was undeniably turned in as the authorities didn't know her family was Jewish. By choice, her father had not reported his family to the census authorities and they did not wear the yellow star.

Shortly afterwards, the Gestapo returned and arrested Flora's mother and her 15-year-old brother Henri. Flora and her other siblings, also present at the house at the time, managed to hide and were not found. Unfortunately, Flora was later arrested and deported to Auschwitz on convoy 70. She then ended up in Bergen-Belsen, where she remembers feeling very close to death just before the liberation of the camp.

Her father, her mother, her brother Henri - in all, twenty members of her family - did not come back. Eight months after the end of the war, Flora returned to Marseille, where no one was waiting for her. Attractive and charming, she chose to stay single despite her many suitors. She did eventually meet true love, but unfortunately, he was married. Nevertheless, at 41, she became pregnant. They had a daughter, whom he recognized.

When I met Flora, she was funny and irresistible, although she admits that for the past ten years, she has been thinking more often about that dark period of her youth. Talking about it causes her blood pressure to rise sharply. But it's important for her to talk, and she can't bear when people tell her it's "ancient history". She also can't help replying sharply to those who claim that "enough is enough" that for her "it will never be enough" because her life without her mother and her family has been forever altered.

(3)

DEPORTATION

Jeanette

It was still early when they marched us from the Gestapo headquarters in Brussels to the train station. We didn't know where we were going—only that we were going. Again.

They loaded us onto a train. At first, it looked like any other passenger train, not a cattle car—not yet. I remember thinking, "Maybe we can jump. Maybe we can run." But there was no chance. A German soldier sat in every car, gripping his rifle, his eyes scanning for any sign of resistance. Just one wrong movement and we'd be gone before we even left Belgium.

We sat packed together, shoulder to shoulder. My friend Sophie clutched my hand. No one spoke. The train creaked forward, and the silence was louder than screams.

There were no windows we could see out of, only the walls and our own thoughts closing in. I tried to count the hours. Then I stopped. The days blurred. Time didn't move in a straight line anymore. Only the train did.

Somewhere along the way, we were transferred to cattle cars. The kind used for animals—filthy, dark, no food, no water, barely air. We were no longer passengers. We were cargo.

The train left Brussels.
Three days later, we arrived in Auschwitz.

Judith

The journey to Auschwitz was a nightmare. We were crammed into a wagon with no space to move, forced to share a single bucket that filled quickly with urine. No one wanted to use it. The air was thick and unbearable. We had no water for days, and people began to lose their minds from thirst—literally losing their minds.

One man, desperate, kept talking about escaping through a tiny window. At first, we thought he wouldn't do it. But after hours of whispering and debating, he jumped. I don't know if he made it or if a train hit him, but I will never forget the desperation we all felt.

David

The day came when they told us we were being transported. We didn't know where—we were just told to line up and wait. Eventually, we were marched to the train yard.

The trains came, and they started loading us into the cattle cars. You couldn't fit more than maybe 50 people, but they crammed in as many as 80. It was so tight, you couldn't sit, you couldn't lie down. We were standing, packed together, falling on top of each other when the train moved.

We were trapped in that cattle car for over two days. They gave us two buckets—one for water, and one for waste. Just two buckets—for all of us. I remember my mother crying. I remember my little sisters crying too. And I remember my older brother, Jacobo, trying to comfort us, whispering words I can't even recall, just trying to keep us from falling apart.

"There was a single bucket of water and one for waste. We had no food, and barely enough space to breathe, let alone sit."

- SAUL -

Julia and her parents.

Hedy

One morning, we were all told to gather. Destination unknown. They packed us into a cattle car—about a hundred people. There was barely any room to sit. The floor was just plain wood, nothing else. I was squeezed in the middle. They threw in a bale of hay, a bucket of water... and that was it. The hay—that was our bathroom.

And so, we traveled. Four days. Four nights.
A lot of people didn't make it.

The infants... they had no milk.
Their mothers—starving, weak—had nothing left to give.
The elderly—one by one—they just...
died.

Julia

On the way to Auschwitz, I had an argument with my father for the last time. He told me, "Julia, you have to live, you have to tell all the horrible things you are going to see." I didn't understand what he was talking about.

I replied, "But what horrible things are you talking about?" "You have to tell!" he said. He had understood that horrible things were coming. When the German Jews came to France and told us about Kristallnacht, how all the store windows had been broken and all the Jewish businesses had been set on fire, my father understood that we were doomed.

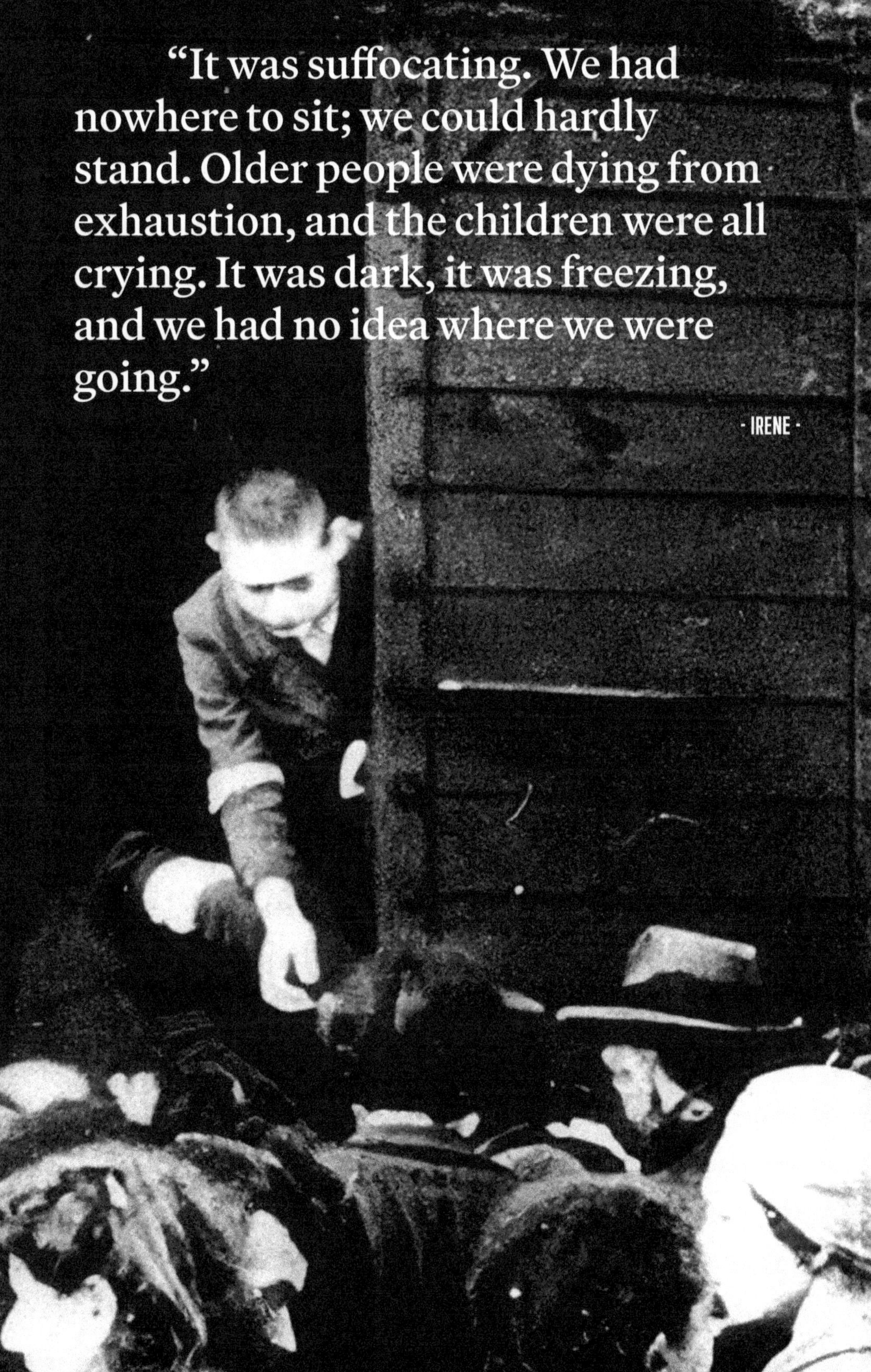

"It was suffocating. We had nowhere to sit; we could hardly stand. Older people were dying from exhaustion, and the children were all crying. It was dark, it was freezing, and we had no idea where we were going."

- IRENE -

Esther

On September 2nd, 1943, they hadn't reached the quota of a thousand people the convoy was intended to have. So, they went to the maternity ward of Rothschild Hospital, where they arrested mothers who had just given birth and their newborns. They found more people to add to the convoy in the retirement home next door. I was part of this atrocious convoy, with women in labor, wailing infants, and dying old people, with no water and an overturned bucket of feces...

"By the time we arrived in Auschwitz, about 25% of the people in that cattle car were either dead or dying. We were barely alive ourselves."

- DAVID -

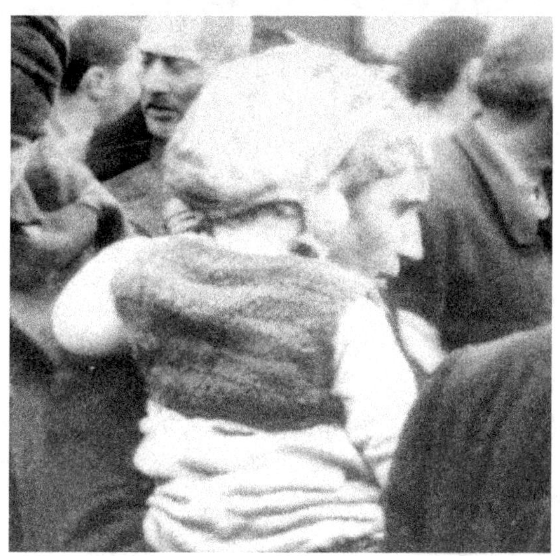

Hedy Fladel

Hedy Fladell was born on January 12, 1931, in Sighet, Romania, into a close-knit Orthodox Jewish family.

As antisemitic laws intensified, life shrank — curfews, yellow stars, and finally, a ghetto built on her very street, its doors and windows boarded so no one could step outside.

In 1944, Hedy and her family were forced into the Sighet Ghetto and soon after deported. The journey to Auschwitz-Birkenau was an ordeal: days locked in an airless cattle car with only a bale of hay and a bucket for provisions, as infants and the elderly faded before her eyes.

At Auschwitz, she was assigned to sweep the camp streets — broom and shovel in hand — clearing paths among the dead. Later, she was transferred to the Mühldorf concentration camp in Germany, where she endured more brutality while clinging to the will to live.

In 1945, Hedy was liberated by U.S. forces in Bavaria. She later immigrated to the United States, where she rebuilt a life out of silence and loss. What struck me most when we met was the profound solitude that surrounds her still — a quiet that speaks of a trauma carried, not told. It lingers in her eyes, in the spaces between her words — the weight of survival, impossible to name but impossible to forget.

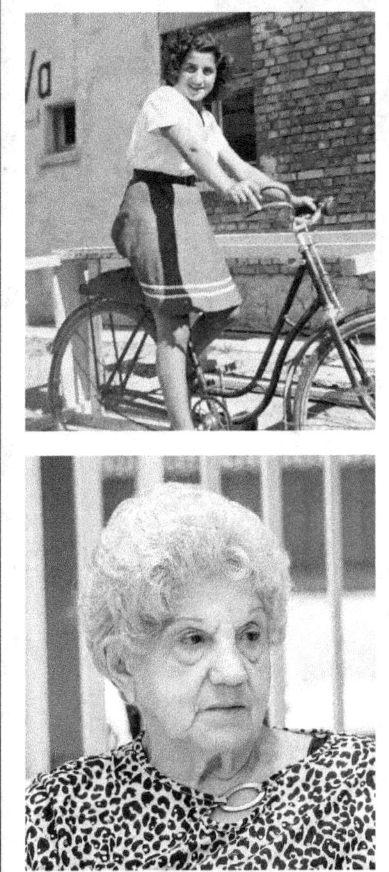

BIOGRAPHIE

Lucette Gejzenblozen

Lucette was born in Paris in 1924, a stone's throw from the Sacré-Cœur. Her parents came from Poland and she had a sister, Sarah, just two years her senior.

During the war, her father, a renowned decorator, took his family to take refuge in Lyon, where he quickly found work. His twin brother came to join them after his wife and four of his children were arrested, none of whom ever returned. He died of grief. Lucette had just turned twenty when she too was arrested, along with her parents. Sarah, who was not at home, escaped deportation. They were taken to the Gestapo, led by Klaus Barbie, where Lucette saw her father beaten up. All three were deported on the very last convoy from Lyon to Auschwitz. They were separated a few days later.

On her release, Lucette is convinced that her parents are dead. However, against all odds, she found her mother, hospitalised in a deplorable condition, but alive. Her father did not survive.

Lucette returned to Montmartre, married and became the mother of three children. Her own mother attended the weddings of her two daughters, but never really recovered from her deportation.

A few years before her death, Lucette was devastated to hear a procession shouting "death to the Jews" outside her windows, and above all to see that no one around her reacted. Lucette accompanied me to a conference at the Shoah Memorial, where I was presenting the episode devoted to her. That day, very moved, she repeated many times that she was fulfilling her mission by bearing witness, but that there were certain things she could never say. Lucette died at the end of 2018, taking the worst of her story with her.

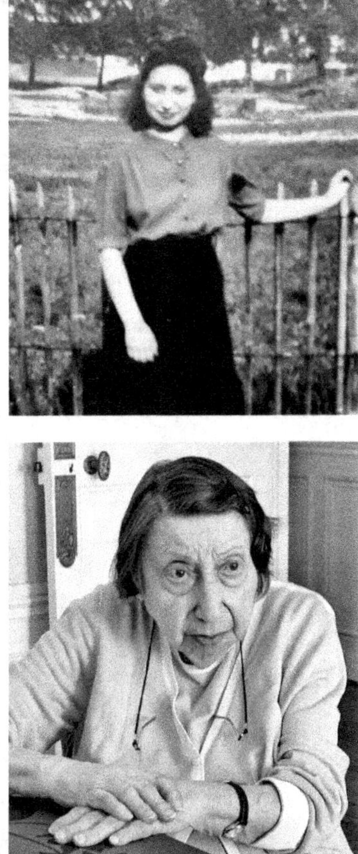

Ginette Kolinka

Ginette was born in Paris in 1925. Her parents had six daughters, of whom Ginette was the youngest before her little brother Gilbert was finally born.

During the war, the family took refuge in Avignon (south of France), a place and time of which Ginette has fond memories. She worked at the local farmer's market with one of her sisters, and at lunchtime, they would take turns going home for lunch. One day, as she arrived home, the Gestapo was there. They took Ginette, her father, her little brother and her nephew Jojo to Drancy. They were then taken to Auschwitz on convoy 71, Simone Veil's convoy.

On arrival, the Germans shouted that the elderly, the people who were tired and the children could go into the trucks that would take them to the camp. Ginette told her father to do so and he climbed into the truck with the two boys. She would never see them again. Selected for work, Ginette was as discreet as possible, avoiding beatings and trouble. Miraculously, she avoided death marches.

Upon her return to Paris, completely unaware of what had become of her mother and sisters, she was surprised to find them in the family apartment. Ginette, who felt she had no emotions left in her, told her mother that her father and the boys had been gassed and burned. She didn't realize the violence such a revelation represented for her mother, who had never heard of a gas chamber or crematorium. Ginette got married, and together they sold hosiery at different local markets for years.

She doesn't allow anyone to think she had any courage at all: for her, luck was the only thing that enabled her to survive. She has one son, two grandsons and is now a great-grandmother. After keeping quiet for decades "for fear of annoying people", she is now a tireless witness, speaking out in schools where she is adored by the students. Yet this woman, who fights hatred relentlessly, finds it hard to believe in the power of her testimony. She feels that after all, we have learned nothing from history.

"Arriving in Auschwitz was like walking into a nightmare"

- SAUL -

(4)

THE ARRIVAL

Hedy

When we arrived in Auschwitz, it was dark. They told us to get off the train, to leave everything behind, to line up. No wait—they didn't tell us. They screamed it at us.

The German shepherds were barking. The SS—hundreds of them—had whips in their hands. And if you didn't move fast enough, if you hesitated for even a second—they whipped you until you fell. And if you fell, you might not get up again.

I was terrified. We all were.

Judith

Soldiers were screaming, "Raus! Out!" as we were chased off the wagon. Chaos surrounded us—people crying, belongings scattered, orders barked without mercy. An old man was being carried, but the soldiers shouted, "Don't carry him, throw him out!" His daughter pleaded for them to spare him, but it made no difference.

We had heard that Auschwitz was a bad place,
but nothing prepared us for its horrors.

Yvette

Once the doors to the car were unlocked, we were told to jump down on the gravel. I started to stretch and take a deep breath. The odor was horrendous. Where was it coming from? We were actually on top of a crematorium—crematorium 2.

What we were smelling was the smell of burnt flesh.

Esther

When they opened the doors, we smelled smoke and saw the kapos—we didn't even know what that meant. Men in striped uniforms, clubs in hand, chased people who looked like skeletons. We were told our life expectancy here could be weeks or even days. I was only 15, how could I imagine my life expectancy to be so short. I was all alone, without my parents, but I kept hoping that I would see them again one day.

Birkenau's ramp. Photo from the Auschwitz Album.

Auschwitz in Poland, was the largest concentration camp complex of the Nazi system. It was made up of three main camps:
Auschwitz I, the barracks;
Auschwitz II–Birkenau,
the killing center;
Auschwitz III–Buna-Monowitz,
the industrial complex.
More than 1.1 million people were murdered there —around one million of them Jews. Only a few thousand survived. The witnesses in this book are among those rare survivors.

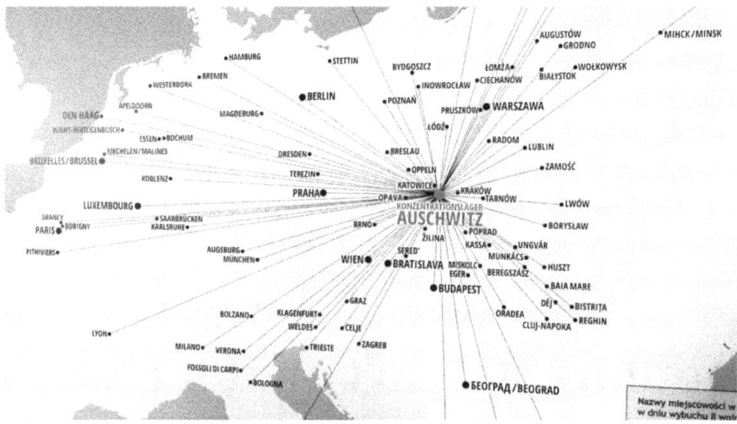

"You see all these convoys arriving from everywhere... Auschwitz turned out to be Europe's most tragically efficient project."

- ELIE -

After the selection, women and children on their way to the gas chamber at Auschwitz-Birkenau
Photo from the Auschwitz Album.

"We were nothing, absolutely nothing, it didn't matter if we were put to death or not. We were just objects, things."

- NICOLAS -

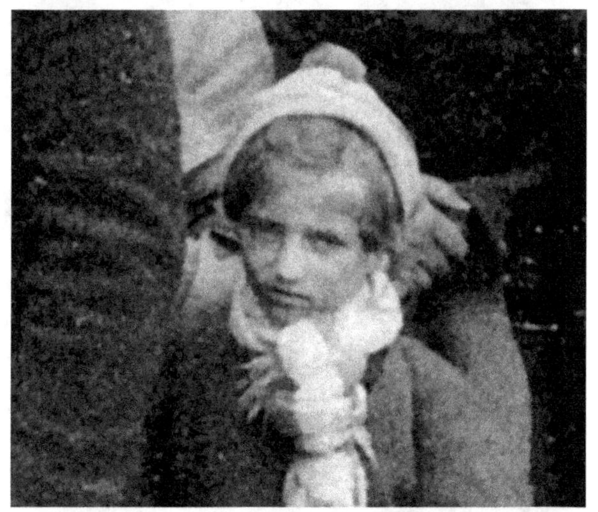

Mothers and children heading to the gas chamber.
Photo from the Auschwitz Album.

The Auschwitz Album is a unique collection of images captured by SS photographers at Auschwitz-Birkenau during the spring and summer of 1944, documenting the arrival, selection, and looting of Hungarian Jewish deportees.

The album was discovered after the war by Holocaust survivor Lili Jacob in an abandoned house in Germany. In the 1960s, she made the album available to the prosecution at the Auschwitz Trial in Frankfurt, and in 1983 she donated it to Yad Vashem, requesting that it remain free of rights for all work dedicated to remembrance.

Léon

As soon as the doors opened, anyone who could jump, did. But there were people of all ages—some couldn't jump, some were pushed to get out faster and broke a leg. Those were thrown onto a truck and taken back into the forest... where they were finished off with machine guns.

Jeanette

When the train stopped, the doors slid open, and the cold rushed in. The air smelled strange—burning, thick, unnatural. I didn't understand what I was smelling. None of us did. A man shouted something in German, his voice sharp and urgent. We didn't know what he was saying, but then, through the chaos, another voice called out. It wasn't a guard—it was one of the prisoners. His voice was rough, but there was something else in it, something desperate.

"You're all over 16, and you want to work!"

He was warning us. He was telling us what to say.

Then his voice changed. "Get out, you lazy people!" He was shouting now, his tone harsher. He had to sound cruel. The SS officers were watching, listening. But his words were not meant to harm us—they were meant to save us.

The shouting never stopped. Orders. Insults. Numbers being called out. More orders.

Ginette [2]

When we arrived at the camp, guards pulled us off the train. I was tall for my age—I didn't look fourteen—and I spoke Yiddish, which sounded like German. So when they asked me in German, "Wie alt bist du?" I panicked and answered "seventeen." It must not have been my time—anyone under sixteen was sent straight to the gas chambers. There, you could smell it. The stench hit me the moment I stepped off the train: burning flesh rising from the chimney.

"The dogs" by Shelomo Selinger.

"There was shouting. Dogs barking. Bright lights. We heard the yell, 'Raus! Schnell!' The soldiers banged on the sides, forcing us to move. I jumped down, my legs were like jelly. People collapsing around me. Mothers clung to their children."

- LEON -

Julia

When we got off the train, we could hear shouting in German and dogs barking. Then a man in a striped uniform whispered to me in French, "Make sure you don't let your father get into the truck." My father was exhausted. When he heard that the trucks were there for people who were too old or tired to walk to the camp, he tried to get in, but I stopped him.

The people who had climbed into the
trucks were never seen again.
They were taken directly to the gas chambers.

Ginette [1]

After arriving at the camp, when we got out of the cattle cars, I was the one who told my father and little brother to get on the trucks. I had heard that it was for people who were tired or sick, so they wouldn't have to walk to the camp, and I said to Daddy and Gilbert: "Go on, get in there!" They did what I said. Obviously, it was because they wanted to. Daddy wouldn't have obeyed his youngest daughter. But in my young mind, it was me who sent them to the gas chambers.

It was, of course, the last time I saw them.

Gilbert, Ginette's younger brother, and their father Léon — both were sent directly to the gas chamber upon their arrival at Birkenau.

Irene

The officers were screaming at us in German, clubs in their hands, with their vicious dogs.

They were yelling, "Get out, you dirty Jews, and make it quick." Before we could even process what was happening, they began the separation—men to one side, women and children to the other.

My mother took my little brother, and I gripped my four-year old sister's hand tight so she wouldn't get lost in the chaos. I saw the chimneys right away. In my innocence, I couldn't believe the Nazis had so many factories that they needed us to come work for them—little did I know we were the daily rations for the gas chamber.

Before I could even let that thought settle, an SS officer cut between my sister and me, and I had to let go of her hand forever. I heard my mother call out, "Don't cry, I will come for you later." That was the last time I heard her voice.

Then we were herded into a vast,
freezing hall, surrounded by strangers. The SS barked:
"Take off your shoes! Strip! Hold your clothes in one hand,
put your valuables in the bin!"

Saul

Arriving at Auschwitz was like walking into a nightmare. It was pure chaos. People were screaming, orders were being barked at us, families were torn apart in an instant. The men were sent one way, women and children the other.

I was only thirteen. But a man in striped pajamas leaned toward my mother and whispered, 'Say he's eighteen, so he can go to work.' In that moment, my mother had to make an impossible choice. She told me to say I was eighteen. That split-second decision likely saved my life.

And it was the last time,
I ever saw my mother and my sisters.

Esther

Of the 1,000 people in our convoy, 106 women and 243 men were chosen for work. We stripped for a cold shower, without soap or towel, then were shaved and tattooed with a number.

"You don't have a name anymore; you are now the number tattooed on your arm. Here, you walk in through the gate and leave through the chimney."

We looked out the window and saw smoke—we'd arrived only an hour earlier, yet they'd already burned 700 people. Those not selected were marched immediately into the billowing crematoria smoke.

Esther.

Hedy

We walked toward a platform where Dr. Mengele stood. He barely looked at us—just waved his stick, right or left, right, left.

Right—you lived.
Left—you died.

The young ones, the strong ones—they went right, for labor. My older sister—she looked healthy, developed—she was sent right. The rest of us—my mother, my sisters, and me—we were sent left. But when I looked at my sister in the other line, she was crying.

I turned to my mother. “I’m going to get her. We should stay together. Why should she be alone?” So I ran. I pushed through. It wasn’t easy, but somehow—I got across. I grabbed her hand. “Come, let’s go back to Mother.”

But we couldn’t go back.

The dogs. The whips. The shouting. Every time we tried to move, they forced us back. After a few tries, I looked up—and I couldn’t see my mother anymore. She was gone. But we thought—we’ll catch up with them later.

There was no later.

My sister and me held on to each other as they pushed us forward. A Jewish Kapo saw me and warned me to lie and say I was 17. I was only 13 and anyone that looked at me could tell I wasn’t 17, but I said it anyway. I don’t think they really cared – the more labor, the better.

Everyone that was sent to the left—they were stripped naked. Herded into the gas chambers. They were told they were going to take showers. Thousands of showerheads. But instead of water, gas came down.

Mothers held their children.
Crying. Screaming.
Watching them take their last breath.

Hedy with her mother and sisters. She was the only one who survived.

Hedy.

“With just a flick of his thumb, he determined who would live and who would die. Left - Death. Right - Work.”

- NISSEN -

Nissen

The moment we arrived in Auschwitz, chaos surrounded us. Guards shouting, dogs barking, and the air was thick with the smell of smoke. I clung to my father's hand as we were pushed into a long line. I didn't know what was happening, but I could feel the fear around me.

Ahead of us, a man sat on a table, chain-smoking, watching, deciding. I would later learn his name—Dr. Josef Mengele. With just a flick of his thumb, he determined who would live and who would die. Left? Death. Right? Work... and then death later.

My father tried to shield me behind him, but Mengele noticed. He stood, stepped toward me, and looked directly into my eyes. "How old are you?" he asked.

I didn't think. I didn't plan.
The words just came out. "Seventeen. I'm 17."
I wasn't. I wasn't even close.

The guards laughed. Mengele smirked. He spoke German, "Ich weiss," that translates to "I know." He knew I was not more than 11."

I wasn't even 11 yet.
He waved his hand dismissively.
"Go back with your father."

I was ten and a half years old.

Then they tattooed me.
Five numbers. 14316.

My name was gone.
My identity erased.
I was no longer a child, or a person.
I was a number.

Léon

And then once we were on the ramp, a member of the Sonderkommando grabbed me by the shoulder and said, "Go with your father." He saved my life. My mother was devastated—they were taking her child away. I didn't know it then, but that was the last time I ever saw her. She was sent straight to the gas chamber.

I walked down to the end of the ramp, where the infamous Dr. Mengele stood—he was making the gesture: death or life. I stood on my tiptoes, right on my father's feet, to look a little taller. And by some miracle, he sent me to the side of the living.

Once selected, I went through disinfection, shaving, and was given the striped uniform. When my father came out, he was completely bald, no hair, nothing left, even his mustache, gone — I could hardly recognize him.

And there we were, entering the camp, still without having eaten anything. We had to wait until the next day to receive a small piece of bread and a foul-colored drink.

David

My mother clutched my little sisters as soldiers beat her toward some giant pits. I stood beside my older brother, Jacobo, watching as they forced our family forward. And then... the machine guns started. I watched them fall into those holes. I heard it. And it never stopped. It just kept going.

Immediately after came the selection, what they called Appell. Someone yelled to Jacobo that I should stand on his two feet so I would look bigger. And I remember my brother was lifting me up and putting me on his feet. I was 11 years and 8 months old—even though under 16, you weren't supposed to make it past the selection at all.

That gesture — it meant life.

Leon

And then—the selections began. A quick motion of the hand—left or right. Men to one side, women to the other. I didn't know it then, but those sent left were walking to their deaths.

When it was my turn, I stood in line as an SS officer with a monocle made his selections. He asked for my profession, and I told him, "I worked with horses." That seemed to pique his interest, and after a brief discussion, they let me pass. That's how they made their decisions—based on what use you could be to them.

Once inside Auschwitz, the process began: first, a shower, then the striped uniform, and finally, the tattoo. They used a foul-smelling liquid to clean my skin before tattooing me with my new identity. My number: 161744.

Jeanette

When we reached a building, they separated us—men to one side, women to the other. I looked for someone I knew, someone familiar, but all I saw were frightened faces.

Inside, they took everything. Our clothes, our shoes. They cut our hair. Some girls screamed when they saw their hair falling to the floor. Others just stood there, frozen.

Then, they gave us the striped dresses. The fabric was thin, stiff. It did nothing to keep out the cold.

And then they gave us numbers.

Mine was 76,655.

The girl who tattooed me whispered, 'I will do it neatly.' She was careful, almost gentle. Some girls weren't so lucky—their numbers were jagged, stretched, uneven. But it didn't matter. We weren't names anymore. We weren't people.

We were numbers.

Saul

The first thing they did was strip us of everything—our clothes, our hair, even our dignity. They shaved our heads, disinfected us like we were nothing more than livestock, and tattooed numbers on our arms. My number was 3913. I wasn't a person anymore; I was just a number.

"Inside, they took everything, our clothes, our shoes. They cut our hair. And then they gave us numbers..."

- JEANETTE-

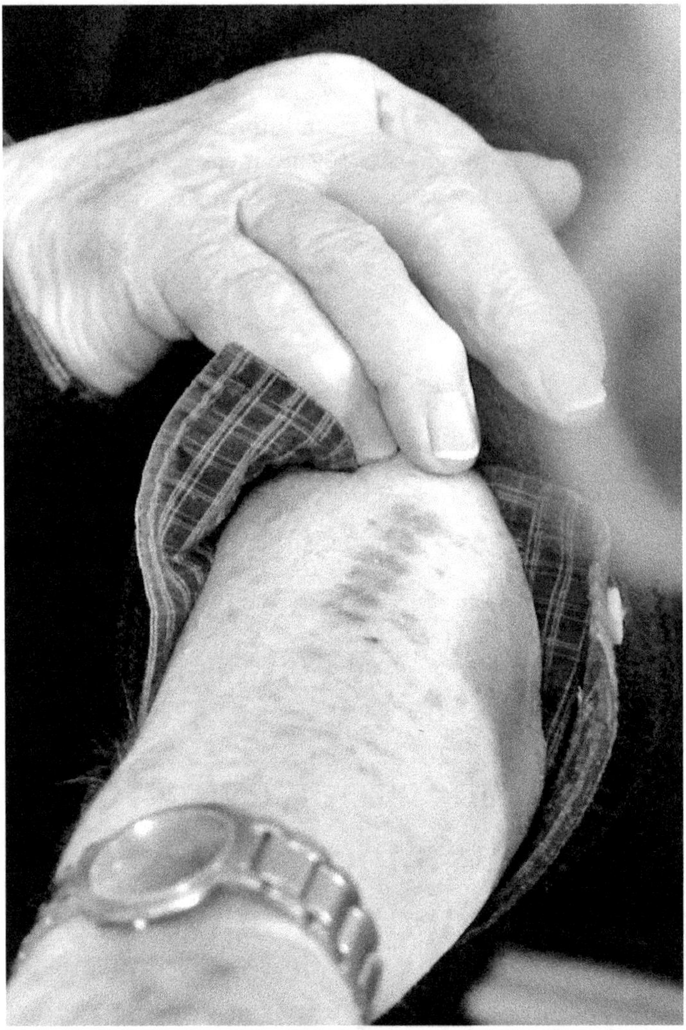

Jacques - 173708.

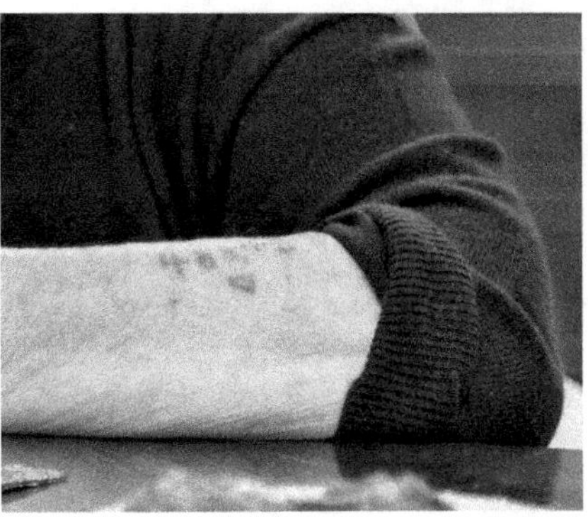

Julia - 46540.

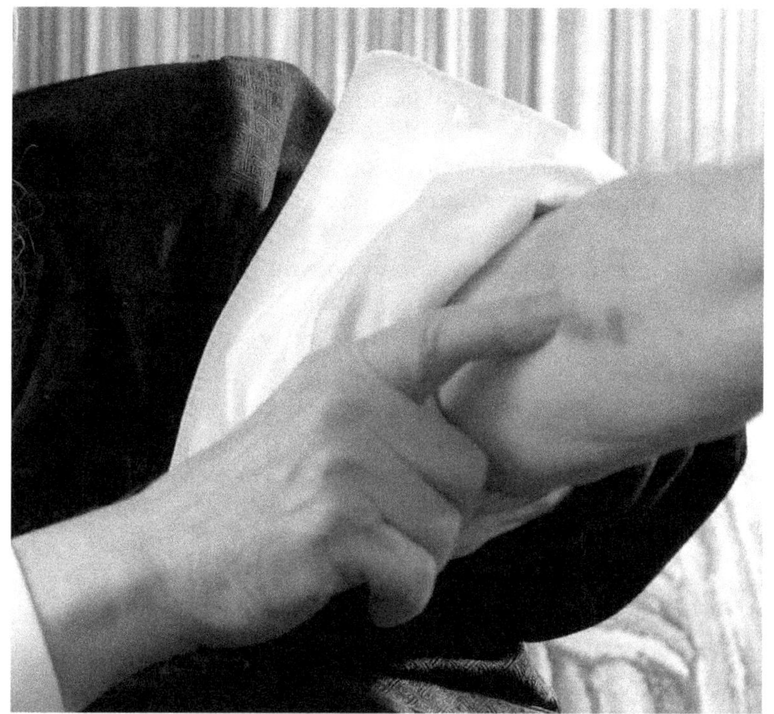

Nissen - 14316.

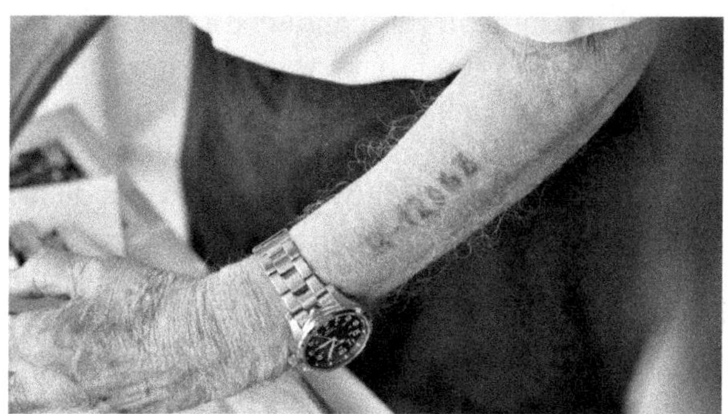

Albert - 12063.

"You don't have a name anymore: you are now the number tattooed on your arm"

- ESTHER -

Ginette [2]

There were several people tattooing numbers. And do you know what they used? Indelible ink and a dip pen. The wounds festered. There was no hygiene. 78660 - I've played those numbers in the lottery many times, but I've never won.

Of the 800 women in my convoy, only 91 were selected to enter the camp. I had never seen a naked body before, except my own. Suddenly, I had to undress completely—bra and underwear included—in front of everyone: young, old, even women whose bodies bore the scars of pregnancies. I was mortified, trying to cover my breasts and pubic area with my hands. That's when they tattooed 78599 on my arm. From that moment on, we were not ourselves anymore.

Then they shaved us with brand-new blades so violently that our heads and pubic areas bled. We staggered to a quick shower—ice-cold water first, then scorching hot—and all of us screamed. No soap. No towels.

They handed out clothes from abandoned suitcases left in the cattle cars. Anything still in good shape was sent to Germany; what was old, stained, and worn fell to us. I ended up with a nightgown, a small sweater, and a skirt. For shoes, I was given one high heel and the other flat. Try walking like that! That was a death sentence. At least the gown's long sleeves spared me from the rough blanket and the filthy bodies pressed against me that first night—We had neither socks nor underwear.

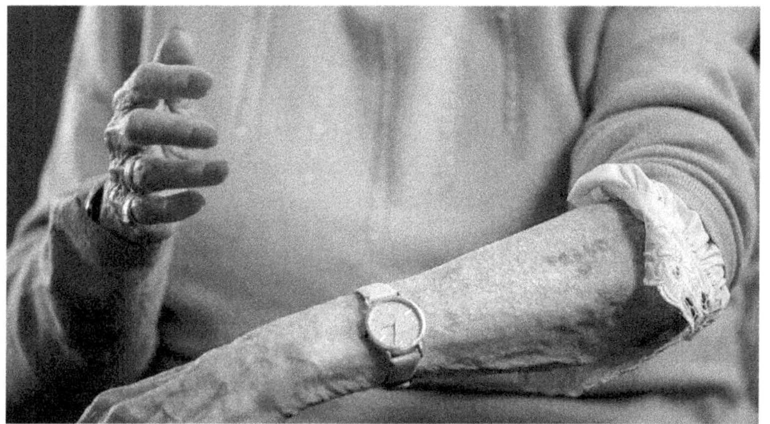

Ginette - 78660.

Frania

We saw men in striped uniforms, with wheelbarrows... I remember one of them told us, “When you go into the shower rooms, you’ll be completely naked. Look up at the showerheads—if water comes out, it means you’ll live a little longer...”

So we stood there, naked, looking up, and it felt like an hour. I don’t know how long it actually lasted, but it seemed like an eternity. Then suddenly, things started moving again. They made us open our mouths to check if we had gold teeth, and after that, we went into the showers. The water came out, and I let out a sigh of relief. We had nothing—no towel, nothing—just a naked body, with nothing at all.

I didn’t have striped clothing; I had a skirt that was too big, a man’s shirt, and men’s shoes that hurt my feet.

They threw clothes at us, randomly. I got an evening dress, with lace-up shoes that had wooden soles—and one of them was missing its lace. It might seem anecdotal, but in the camp, that meant a death sentence. Sometimes as you were walking, they would suddenly shout, “Run!” And if you were ordered to run and couldn’t, it meant certain death.

Irene

Then I found myself in a vast, freezing hall, surrounded by strangers. The SS ordered us: “Take off your shoes! Strip! Hold your clothes in one hand, put your valuables in the bin!”

And then it hit me—my mother’s diamonds.

I started searching my skirt. I found four. I didn’t know how many she’d sewn in, but I didn’t have time to look for more. I had no clothes to hide them, nowhere to keep them safe. And I knew—if they searched me, if they found them, they would shoot me on the spot.

There was only one choice. I took a deep breath, placed the diamonds in my mouth, and swallowed. They slid down my throat and I felt something strange in that moment. I felt free.

Leon

After the selection, I went through disinfection, then they shaved me and gave me those striped clothes. My father came out after his turn—his head was completely shaved, no hair, not even his mustache. I had a hard time... I didn't recognize him. Then we were brought into the camp. We still hadn't eaten anything. We had to wait until the next day to get a small piece of bread and some foul colored drink.

Lucette : "This is the outfit my mother came back from the camp in.
It carried the smell of that place — of rotten fish.
Everything there seemed rotten, even the water we drank.
I had to wash it many times before the smell finally went away."

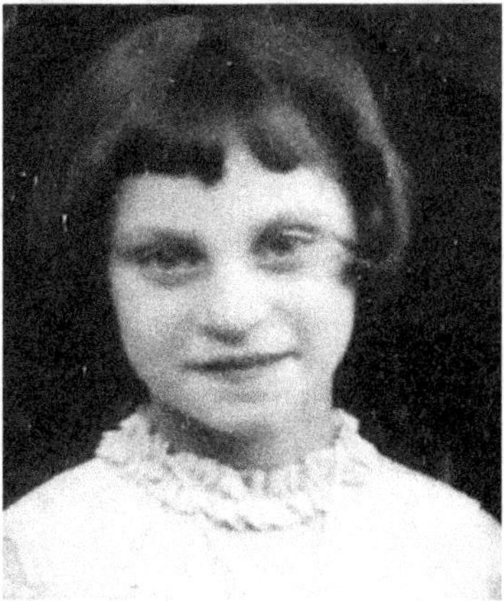

Yvette Levy

Born in 1926 from Alsatian parents, Yvette grew up in the suburbs of Paris in a close-knit family of three children.

As a member of the Éclaireurs Israélites de France (French Jewish scouting organization), she was arrested with her group on July 21, 1944. She was just 18 years old. She was sent to Drancy, then to Auschwitz, on convoy 77, the last one to leave France. For this modest young woman, finding herself naked in front of men and seeing all those naked women's bodies around her was a very uncomfortable feeling. She spent a year in deportation, first in Birkenau, then in a camp in Czechoslovakia, which was quickly abandoned by the Nazis and from which she left to find her way home on her own.

When she finally arrived in Paris, at the Lutetia Hotel, she knew nothing of her parents' fate, not even if they had been arrested. She sent a telegram to their address, like throwing a bottle in the sea. When Yvette's mother came to meet her, Yvette didn't recognize her. She was thin and her hair had turned all white. As for Yvette, she weighed 36 kilos (79 pounds) and was also unrecognizable. Eventually, the two women fell into each other's arms and left the hotel together by subway for home. When Yvette's father first saw her, he didn't recognize her. So as not to cause them any more pain, Yvette didn't tell her parents anything about what she had gone through. However, she was one of the first former deportees to talk about her experiences, keeping the promise she had made to herself in the camp.

After the war, Yvette was concerned that no man would want to marry her, a deportee who was traumatized by her close encounters with death. But five years later, she married Robert Lévy, with whom she had a daughter. Yvette feels now that her trauma affected her daughter more than she expected. She devotes much of her time and energy to sharing her experiences.

Léon Lewkowicz

Léon Lewkowicz was born in 1930 in Łódź, Poland.

He was a true miracle to his parents, who had waited many years to have a child — his mother was over forty when he was born. During the early years of his life, the two were inseparable.

On his first day of school, Léon was attacked by classmates who pulled down his pants to see if he was Jewish. He returned home in tears, and his mother decided to keep him close, becoming his teacher herself.

At the age of ten, the family was forced to leave everything behind and enter the Łódź Ghetto. Léon slept in a suitcase under a bed. He remembers that in the ghetto there was no trash — people were so hungry they ate absolutely everything. Death was part of daily life.

At fourteen, he arrived at the Birkenau camp, where he miraculously survived the selection by lying about his age, since all children under sixteen were sent directly to the gas chamber. Léon narrowly escaped that fate — one of the very few to emerge alive from a gas chamber during the Sonderkommando revolt of October 7, 1944. He later said he had "known hell while still alive."

Liberated at Buchenwald, he was among the 426 child survivors received by the Œuvre de Secours aux Enfants (OSE) in June 1945, alongside Élie Buzyn.

After the war, weighing only thirty kilos, he decided to build up his body and learn to fight so that no one would ever call him a "dirty Jew" again. In 1955, he became the French weightlifting champion, and in 1978 was named Best Craftsman of France (Meilleur Ouvrier de France) as a master jeweler and stone setter.

He later married the woman he affectionately called his "dragonfly."

In 2024, Léon carried the Olympic flame through the streets of Paris — a living symbol of resilience and strength.

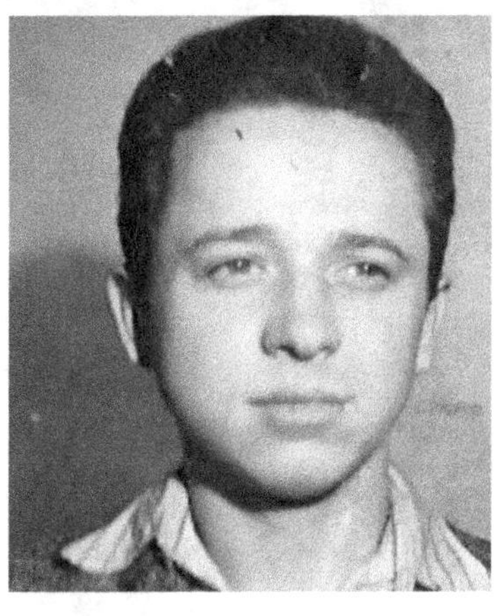

(5)

SURVIVING IN AUSCHWITZ

“Do you see the smoke coming out of the chimney?”

Nicolas

On the second or third day, I asked another deportee, “When will I see my parents again? “He answered, “Your parents? But how old were they?” I replied in the present tense, “My father is 65 years old and my mother 57.” He then looked at me, pointed to the sky and replied: “Do you see the smoke coming out of the chimney? Your parents are there, gone up in smoke.”

At first, I thought it was a tasteless joke...

Then as the days went by and the smoke, with the odor of burnt flesh persisted, I began to wonder whether what I had been told was true.

“We’re all going to go through this”

Julia

After a few days at Birkenau, by the greatest of coincidences, I ran into my favorite cousin, who had been there for a few months already. Before she was deported, she was so beautiful, she wanted to be in the movies. When I saw her, I didn’t recognize her. A skeleton came up to me. It was her. The crematorium ovens were working, and flames were coming out of them. I remember what she told me as she pointed at the chimney: “Listen carefully, Julia. That’s where we’re all headed, if you want to have the slightest chance to survive, you must always go to work. Even if you are tired, even if you are sick, never stay in your barracks.” The barracks were where we slept. She wasn’t the kind to make up stories, so I believed her. It’s partly that which saved my life. One night, a month or two after my arrival, my cousin disappeared. I cried a lot.

I contracted typhus and became gravely ill. I knew that the evening would be the worst and that I would have severe diarrhea. But I followed my cousin’s advice and even then, I never missed one day of work.

Leon

Every day, the gas chambers operated without pause. Death was literally everywhere. Birkenau wasn't a place where you stayed long. You either died there, or they sent you somewhere else.

The living conditions were beyond brutal. We were shoved into barracks meant for horses—about 400 of us packed so tightly that there was barely room to move. Eight to a box, with nothing but straw to sleep on. It was freezing in the winter, suffocating in the summer. And as for food—you couldn't even call it that. Weak, bitter coffee in the morning, a thin, watery soup in the evening.

And the latrines at Birkenau—they were a nightmare: barely functioning, filthy, and dangerous. People would hide there during selections, hoping to avoid the SS officers. The smell was unbearable.

Jacques

There were three levels. We slept six or eight to a bunk, on straw, with no blankets. We were packed so tightly against one another that we couldn't even move or turn over.

In winter it was freezing, and in summer unbearably hot — especially on the top level. But on the bottom, you could get the waste from the others falling on you.

Sometimes, in winter,
we covered ourselves with the bodies of the dead.

A barrack.

"In the latrines, we went one pressed against the other — sometimes on top of each other.

We had to go very quickly; the Kapo was there with his stick."

- JACQUES -

Ginette [1]

The latrines were disgusting and we had no underwear. Can you imagine? We would pee, we had diarrhea due to lack of hygiene. I don't remember ever washing myself when I was there. I was only disinfected a few times.

Now that I say that I wonder how we ever managed.

Jacques

This here was the latrines. We sat side by side, pressed against each other, with water running underneath, and there was a "chief of the latrines" with a stick. We had to go fast — sometimes we ended up one on top of another.

The stench was unbearable, here and everywhere in the camp. When you arrived, you took one shower — and that was the last. But after a few months, you didn't even notice the smell anymore.

The crematoria were smoking ; the air reeked of death.
They say that even 12 to 18 miles away,
you could smell the burning bodies.

Jeanette

Leslie: “What about the food there?”
Jeanette: “Food ? What food?”

Food was nearly nothing. A small piece of bread, a bowl of thin soup. If you were lucky, you got a potato peel floating in it. I learned tricks—if you waited, the heavier parts settled at the bottom of the pot, and you could get more. Small tricks. Small ways to survive.

At night, we lay side by side on the wooden bunks—five, sometimes six to a level. No space. No warmth. Just bodies pressed together, trying to stay alive.

That’s what life in the camp was. Hunger. Cold. Work. The fear of being noticed. The fear of being forgotten. The fear of not surviving another day.

Irene

We had very little to eat ... to say the least. We would get a cup of soup—that's what they called it, but the soup had nothing in it. It was like water, with maybe a piece of potato peel or something in it. Once a day we were allowed to go to the latrine.

I had no problem finding my mother's diamonds that I had hidden during the selection by swallowing them - since I had no solid food; everything that came out was just liquid.

It would've been safer for me to just throw them away. It's not like I was going to buy anything with those diamonds in the camp! But I couldn't. I couldn't let them go. They were the last thing I had from my mother, so I held on to them.

I did it again. And again.

Each time, I recovered the diamonds, cleaned them as best as I could, and swallowed them once more.

It became a ritual
I carried them inside me, over and over,
until the next time...

Irene shows us the diamonds her mother gave her — the ones she managed to keep by swallowing them. Today, they're set in a pendant that she still wears around her neck.

"The call" By Shelomo Selinger

Appelplatz German for "roll call square", the place in concentration camps where prisoners were forced to stand, often for hours, to be counted under extreme conditions(Shelomo's drawing).

David

A day in Auschwitz always started with Appell—the roll call. At six o'clock sharp, they would force us out of sleep, shouting at us to get up.

We stumbled out of the barracks and stood in lines, standing still, waiting to be counted. They would count us over and over again. It could take hours. Then we marched. Every day, at least three kilometers to work. It didn't matter if you were sick, hungry, or exhausted. You marched, or they made you march.

Ginette 2

We slept in barracks, and in each barrack were "coyas"—wooden bunks. Six of us squeezed into one. When one person turned, everyone had to turn.

At dawn, the kapo would enter: "Aufstehen!"—"Get up!" We had to dress quickly, wash if we could, and rush outside for roll call. We could be left standing there for three hours, morning and evening. Some collapsed dead on the spot. That was just how it was.

Nicolas

Every day, you would discover new things. For example, solidarity existed only among people who spoke the same language. There were four of us Hungarian Jews, but to the others we didn't exist. We were nothing, absolutely nothing. It didn't matter if we were put to death or not, we were just objects, things.

I was shocked to discover that people over there found it normal to survive only a day, a week, a month...

Jeanette

In Auschwitz, there was no morning. There was only darkness and the sound of orders being shouted.

We were woken at four o'clock, dragged from sleep into the freezing air. Roll call—Appell—was the first thing, always. We stood outside, lined up in rows, motionless. The cold bit through the thin fabric of our dresses. It didn't matter if it rained or snowed. If someone collapsed, they were beaten. If they didn't get up, they were dragged away. We never saw them again.

After Appell, we worked. I carried heavy stones back and forth, over and over, even when there was no point to it. That was the point—exhaustion. To break us.

Esther

We quickly settled into the nightmare of our daily life. We told ourselves that we were all going to die. After a while, we learned to recognize the warning signs of death: in the evening, when we saw someone becoming bloated, we would whisper, "This one won't last through the night." The next day, we would haul away the corpses.

I made up my mind that I could not die at 15, that I had to go home. It became a mantra for me.

Finally, out of the 106 women from my convoy who went to the camp, only two of us survived.

“The Orchestra” by Shelomo Selinger.

Orchestras From the moment the camp opened, prisoner orchestras were organized to punctuate the rhythm of each day — initially improvised, later more elaborate.

Music could be heard during roll call, at the prisoners' departure for work and their return — all carried out to the sound of military marches, in rows of five. It accompanied executions, and on Sundays, it was played to entertain the Nazis and their families.

Albert, musician.

“I’m a professional guitarist, but fortunately, at the music conservatory I also learned to play the clarinet — and in the end, that’s what saved my life.”

- ALBERT -

Albert

When I was in Auschwitz, I worked as a bricklayer. One day, someone came looking for musicians. He said to us: "The musicians must go to block 5." The Nazis wanted to put together a new camp orchestra.

Before the war, I had learned to play the guitar, but this skill was useless at the camp. Luckily, one of my teachers at the music conservatory had advised me to learn a wind instrument as well. I chose the clarinet and it's ultimately what saved my life.

I went to block 5, where I auditioned, and was hired as a clarinet player for the Auschwitz orchestra. In the morning, we would get up before the others to be ready to play as they left for work, five abreast, to the sound of military music. We did the same in the evening when they returned. In the meantime, in the afternoon, we had to rehearse in a large room for the Sunday concerts, where we would entertain the SS and their families.

Ginette 2

When we marched out of the camp, there was music. No joke. A real orchestra. We had to march in step. And me? I've always been terrified of dogs. If I see a big dog, I cross the street. But there, we were guarded by them—massive dogs. And the guards? Their pleasure was beating us. I got hit with a rifle butt because I picked up a potato peel from the mud. I remember them

walking around with a pot of soup—it was nothing, just murky water. That's all we got. And bread? A loaf this big, for eight people. One thin slice per person. For the entire day.

We didn't have the strength to speak. Barely enough to breathe. I was completely out of it—I didn't even know where I was.

I wasn't living, just barely surviving.

Jacques

I was part of a kommando, called Kanada, a kind of a "welcoming committee." I worked on the ramp, the place where deportees would get off the trains. We wore clean clothes, a striped outfit and a little hat. We looked presentable; we appeared to be in good shape. In fact, we were like extras in a fake show—just part of a setup to reassure the newcomers.

After the deportees left the trains, we would empty the cars. We would take all the packages, and when we found food, we would devour it right away. We also had to unload the dead bodies.

I did this job for ten months, every day. I must have seen about 300,000 people pass before my eyes, people who would later be killed. Then one day, among the crowd, I saw my maternal grandparents who had been deported from Czechoslovakia in July. I wanted to go with them, and it took three of my friends to stop me. One of them said, "If you move, I'll knock you out." My grandmother used to play the piano and loved opera. When I was little, she used to take me to the opera house regularly.

Jacques Altmann recounting, on site, what he lived through in Birkenau.

"I saw about 300,000 people pass through — all sent directly to the gas chamber."

- JACQUES -

“As members of the **Kanada** kommando, we were used as extras — a little healthier-looking than the others , to reassure the new arrivals and prevent uprisings.”

Jeanette

Somehow, I was chosen to work in Kanada. It was the best place to be in Auschwitz. That's what they said. And maybe it was. But it didn't feel like it.

In Kanada, we sorted the belongings of those who arrived—the suitcases, the clothes, the treasures people had clung to as they stepped onto the trains, believing they were starting a new life. Jewelry, watches, family photos. I remember seeing a tiny pair of baby shoes once, neatly packed away in a small bag. I felt sick.

We weren't supposed to keep anything, but some girls tried. A piece of bread. A scarf. If the SS caught you, it meant death. But we found ways to resist. If I saw a good coat, I tore the lining so it wouldn't be sent to Germany.

It was a small act, but it was something.

David

My job was to work on the axles of the train cars. I had to clean the wheels and then grease them up. I'd go to pick up the canisters of grease, but the SS wouldn't make it easy for me. They would always give me the biggest canister they could find. It was twice as heavy as the others. I could barely lift it.

And those cars kept coming, one after another, filled with more and more people every day. People who had no idea what was coming. No clue they were about to walk into hell.

Hedy

My job was to clean the streets. They gave me a broom and a shovel for that. I was sweeping between the bodies. They were everywhere on the ground... there were so many, they didn't even have time to burn them all.

I saw the men forced to dig mass graves. I watched as they threw in the bodies—one after another, after another. Babies. Mothers. Young kids. And when the graves were full, they covered them with dirt. Like they were nothing.

But I saw. I saw everything. It was hell. Then winter came. Winter was horrible in Poland. And worse in Auschwitz.

We didn't have proper clothes. We didn't have proper shoes. Mine were too small, and with the holes in them, my feet were frozen. I couldn't feel my toes anymore. The cold cut through my skin like knives.

And still, I had to sweep.

I spent my days sweeping. Sweeping the alleys of Auschwitz, back and forth, over and over again.

That was my task. And it made no sense. Everything was filthy. The ground was dirt and mud. What was the point?

One day, as I was working, I noticed a truck parked nearby. I got closer to see who was inside.

On Sundays, sometimes, families would come to visit the SS officers who worked in the camp. Women with their children—well dressed, well fed—coming to see their husbands, their fathers.

These sick men—they were proud of what they had done – what they were doing. Their families came not just to visit but to see us. Like we were animals in a zoo.

And then, a group of little children spotted me. They pointed at me, laughing. "Schwein!" they called me. "Pig!"

That day, I understood something.
Hatred—it starts young.

Henri

In Auschwitz 1, I ended up in block 7, where our barracks leader was raving mad. He was terrible. At night, when he couldn't sleep, he amused himself by watching us. When we got up to relieve ourselves, he made us go to the attic, where the windows were wide open. There, in the middle of winter, with subzero temperatures, he would undress us, throw buckets of ice-cold water on us and ask us to "exercise," as he called it. We had to bend our legs, stretch our arms in front of us, and jump. We were naked, freezing, and starving.

We knew we were going to die soon.

That's what we were repeatedly told. "Here, you will leave by the chimney of the crematorium." We were there, living what could have been our last days, and he was throwing water at us and beating us.

Henri shows us what the so-called "sport" he was forced to do in Auschwitz looked like.

"In subzero temperatures, he made us undress, throw buckets of ice-cold water on us, and ordered us to 'exercise,' as he called it — bending our legs, stretching our arms forward, and jumping."

- HENRI -

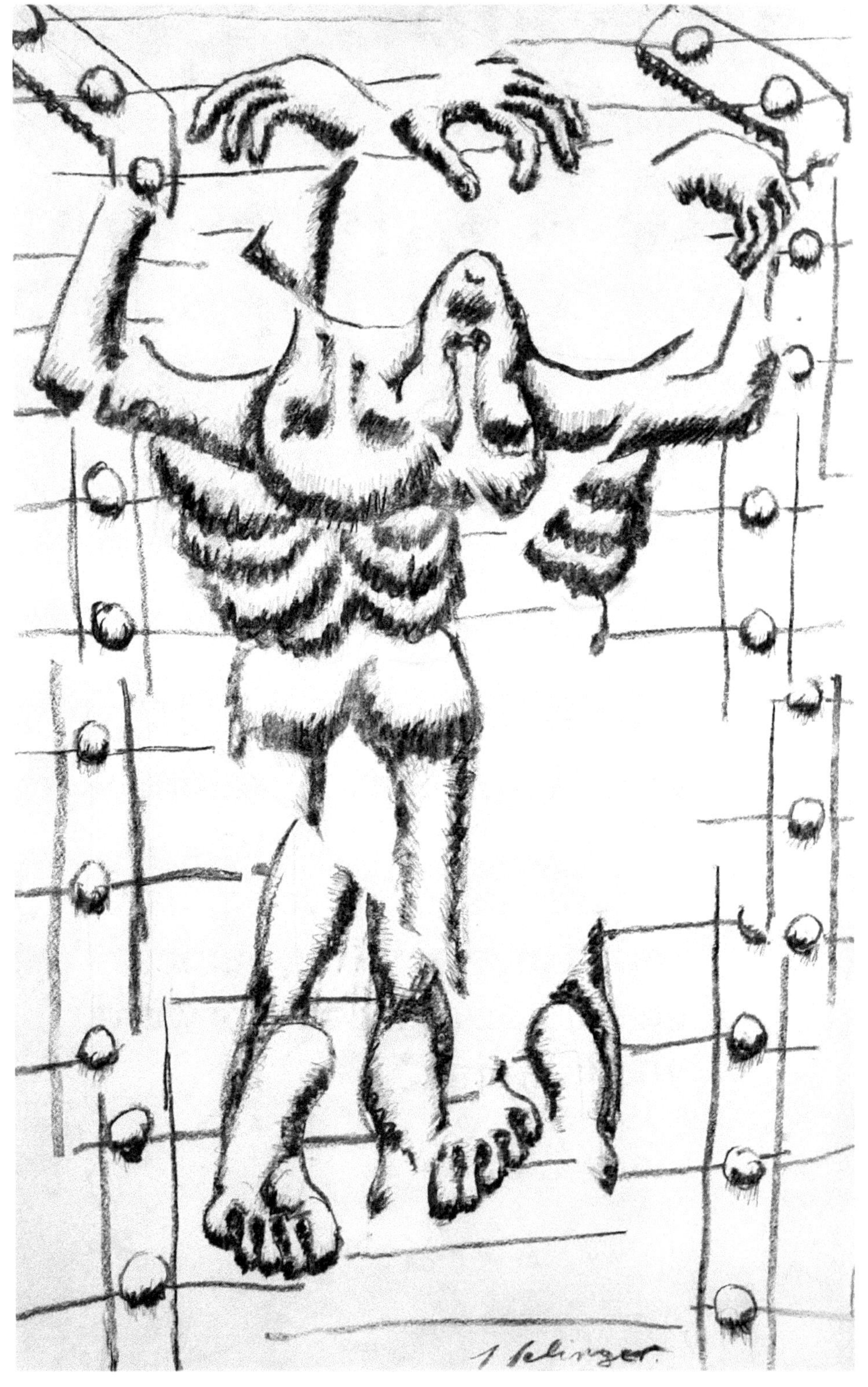

Julia

In my barrack, there was a pregnant woman. Her pregnancy didn't show when she arrived at the camp, but she ended up giving birth there. During labor, we kept an eye on the door, but unfortunately, after the baby was born, an SS man heard the newborn's piercing cry. He forced his way into the room, hitting us with the butt of his rifle. He took the baby and threw it up into the air, just like in pigeon shooting – you throw the pigeon up in the air and you shoot it.

The poor mother survived and returned to Paris at the end of the war because she had another child waiting for her there, but she lost her mind.

Frania

There were several camps within Auschwitz, separated by barbed wire. Our camp was next to a men's camp. One day, a man shouted a name, and a woman from our group started running toward him—she must not have known that the wire was electrified. She put her hands on it and was electrocuted.

"The suicide" by Shelomo Selinger.
In the camp, they called it "Going to the thread" — meaning committing suicide by throwing oneself onto the electrified fences.

Nissen

One morning, I was sick and exhausted, so I didn't go to work. I was so weak. The kapo came over and started beating me—punching, kicking. I collapsed to the ground.

They took me to the clinic. A doctor looked at me, opened my jacket, and saw my chest. Scarlet fever. Highly contagious. My fever was so high, I was delirious. I didn't even know what was happening to me.

The next day, they sent me to Lager F—where Mengele and his doctors did their experiments. There, I saw them. A whole colony of over a hundred dwarfs, all religious Jews. The experiments they did on them, it was terrible.

And then Mengele walked in.
He looked around. And then—he saw me.

"I want to make an experiment on him," he told the other doctors. I looked right into his eyes, just like I'm looking into yours now. And I screamed. "Experiment on monkeys! Not on me!"

You just can't imagine who Mengele was in Auschwitz. Even the highest-ranking Gestapo were afraid of him. He was like a god there. He always had a revolver on his belt. A pistol. I was sure—he was going to shoot me.

Not listening to Mengele...
that was the worst thing you could do.

But he wasn't expecting this. He wasn't expecting me to scream at him like that.For a moment—just a moment—he hesitated. They all looked at each other. A minute, maybe two. But in that moment, it felt like an hour.

And then... he just walked out.

Mengele, known as "the Angel of Death," was a doctor infamous for conducting horrific "medical" experiments on deportees — mainly on twins, and on people with dwarfism or physical deformities. He was responsible for an incalculable number of deaths at Auschwitz.

Irene

Dr. Mengele selected me a few days after I arrived. He needed guinea pigs for his experiments. Mengele put us in one of those dungeons. They were very small and there were five of us, so we were all really close. The first experiment was to find a way to change the color of our eyes. He would inject something into our eyes. He tested so many times, that even decades later, I have two permanent holes. He would inject me under my nails too—sometimes up to twelve times a day. I never knew what it was, what he was putting into me. He wanted to change the color of my eyes. He wanted all of Germany to have blue eyes.

His obsession with the Aryan race knew no limits.

The last experiment he did on me was to remove the number. He needed to figure out how to remove the ink because the SS were tattooed with the same ink under their left arm. When they knew they were losing the war, Mengele didn't want them to be recognized by the Americans or the Russians. If they kept their tattoos, they could be identified, so he experimented on us.

My wounds from these experiments never fully healed, and I still get infections. "Can you imagine someone opening your hand without anesthetics?" The blood was gushing everywhere. When I woke up, a nurse was holding my hand, trying to stop the bleeding.

Then I heard Mengele say, "Send her to the gas chambers!"

- IRENE -

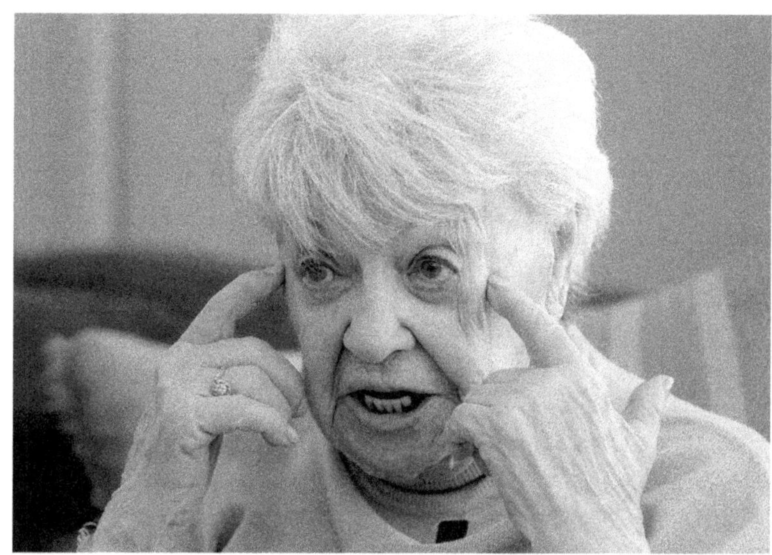

"Mengele would inject something into our eyes, to change their color."

Jeanette

The shouting started before dawn. Orders, whistles, the crack of rifle butts against wooden doors.

The Germans were panicked. We could see it in the way they moved—rushed, uncertain. The war was closing in on them. We didn't know exactly what was happening, but we knew enough. They were emptying the camp. We were being sent somewhere else.

We were given whatever shoes we could find. Some had wooden clogs, some had torn fabric tied around their feet. It didn't matter. Nothing kept out the cold.

It was January 1945. The coldest winter they had seen. The snow covered everything.

And then we walked.

Hour after hour. Day after day. There was no food, no water. Just the sound of boots crunching in the snow. If you slowed down, you were shot. If you fell, you didn't get back up. The guards didn't need to drag bodies away—the snow took care of that.

I held onto Ruth. She was my friend, and in that march, she was the only thing keeping me alive. 'Just one more step,' we whispered to each other. 'Just one more.' That's how we survived—one step at a time.

Élie

On a frigid day in January 1945, as we were coming back from work, SS guards came into our barrack and told us: "It's over, the camp is being evacuated, take your things and get out." We started to gather the few personal items we had left and went outside. We started walking in the cold, in the dark, five abreast, just like when we went to work, in long columns, surrounded by SS men on horses with clubs and rifles. Anyone who showed the slightest sign of fatigue or weakness was shot on the spot. There were bodies scattered all along the road.

We walked like this in subzero temperatures, wearing our light prisoner uniforms with makeshift shoes. Around midnight, we were sent to rest for a few hours in a barn. We had only snow to eat. I don't remember how many days this lasted.

Léon

One morning, there was what I later called a "sporting selection." We woke up, and the block chief, who felt like having some fun, had invented a so-called athletic challenge as an excuse for a selection. I was too small to make it through, so I was automatically chosen to be sent to the gas chamber.

Then Mengele came to inspect those of us marked for death. He looked at me and asked my age. I told him I was sixteen. He gave me a look that clearly said he didn't believe me.

So I repeated, "I'm sixteen — I'm just small for my age."
And then he said, almost casually, "You'll always be small."
That meant only one thing — this was your last hour.

They took us to the gas chamber. We were completely undressed and stood waiting for our turn to die, pressed against one another. Everyone looked at each other in silence.

A gas chamber is long and dark; all you see are the showerheads on the ceiling — meant to make us believe we were going to be disinfected, to be washed. It was a nightmare vision.

There must have been nearly two thousand people inside — women holding newborns, pregnant women, everyone trying to climb higher, gasping for air.

Then suddenly we heard shouting, gunfire — we didn't understand what was happening. The doors burst open, and some of us were pulled out of the chamber. In the courtyard, German soldiers were firing everywhere. Someone shouted, "It's the revolt — the revolt of the Sonderkommandos!"

It was October 7, 1944.
The only revolt in the camp. And it's thanks to that revolt that I'm standing here before you today.

I am a miracle.

The Sonderkommando, composed mainly of Jewish deportees, were assigned to the killing center. Their task was to handle the belongings left behind by the victims in the gas chambers and to transfer their bodies to the crematoria. They themselves were regularly executed and replaced. **On October 7, 1944**, a group of them rose up in revolt. The uprising was brutally crushed, but its symbolic power endures — a desperate act of resistance in the heart of death itself.

Nissen Mangel

Nissen Mangel was born in Bratislava, Slovakia, and spent his earliest years in a warm, observant home — a childhood of faith, family, and ritual until the Nazi invasion shattered it.

In 1944, at just ten and a half, Nissen was deported to Auschwitz with his family, becoming one of the camp's youngest prisoners. There, he survived selections and several face-to-face encounters with Dr. Josef Mengele. On the ramp, Mengele demanded his age; Nissen answered as an adult. Later, in the clinic, when doctors prepared him for an "experiment," he refused to submit — locking eyes with Mengele and protesting. Mengele hesitated, then turned and walked away.

He went on to endure four more concentration camps and a winter death march before liberation in early 1945. He was the only member of his family to survive Auschwitz.

In the years that followed, Nissen rebuilt a life from the ruins — becoming a rabbi, scholar, and teacher devoted to passing on both the history and the responsibility that comes with it.

Decades later, for his 90th birthday, he returned to Auschwitz with about 100 family members — his wife, children, grandchildren, and great-grandchildren — standing together on the same tracks where he had once arrived alone.

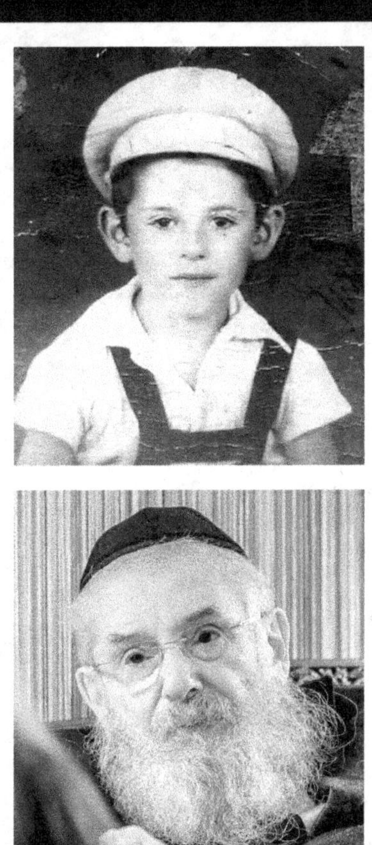

Sarah Montard

Born in Poland in 1928, Sarah emigrated to France with her parents two years later. When the war broke out, Sarah was 11 years old and had just passed the entrance exam for middle school. However, this brilliant student had to give up the idea of studying any further, as her parents sent her to the south of France for her safety. She stayed there for a year, then returned to Paris, where she was arrested with her mother during the Vel' d'Hiv round-up. Realizing that something terrible was afoot, they both managed to escape.

For two years, they hid in Paris. Sarah, who wanted to be a doctor, continued her studies. One morning, at seven o'clock, just as she was about to leave for school, two policemen turned up to arrest them; the two women had been turned in. This time, there was no way of escaping; it was Drancy and then Auschwitz, on convoy 75. Together, they survived the 'death march' to Bergen-Belsen, where Sarah caught typhus. Her fever rose very high and her mother nursed her to health day and night for eight days.

Sarah says her mother gave birth to her twice, at birth and after she almost died from typhus. When they left the camps, they went back to Paris but were unable to get their apartment back. So, they stayed with an aunt. Sarah remembers how she and her mother were given what she thought was an excessive amount of food. Something else from that time stayed in her memory: people refused to listen to their stories. "You have to forget" they were told. But how could they forget when they found out that the police officers who had arrested them had been awarded the Fourragère d'honneur, the medal for heroes of the Resistance? Miraculously, she was then reunited with her father.

In 1952, Sarah got married to Philippe Montard, with whom she had two children. She would have liked to have had six children, but after the birth of the second child, her doctor said that her body couldn't' handle another pregnancy due to the damage she had endured in the camps. As someone who had been sent to her death, giving life was essential.

She named her daughter Claire, in tribute to a comrade who never came back. Being a great-grandmother today is her "ultimate nose-thumbing" at Hitler.

Nicolas Roth

Nicolas was born in Hungary in 1928 into a family of five children. His parents thought they were safe, but in March 1944, the Nazis invaded the country. In a matter of days, their lives were turned upside down. Sensing that the end of the war was close, the Nazis stepped up the pace of the deportation of the Hungarian Jews.

In about seven weeks, over 435,000 people were deported to Auschwitz, the vast majority of whom did not even enter the camp and were sent straight to the gas chambers. Nicolas was deported with his father, mother and youngest sister, the only siblings who had not left the country for Paris. At selection, he was separated from his parents and sister. When, a few days later, he asked where they were, he was shown the smoke coming out of the chimneys. It would take him a few days to realize that what he at first found unbelievable was the truth. The few Hungarians in the camp were poorly regarded by the other prisoners, with whom communication was difficult.

In spite of everything, Nicolas survived seven months in Auschwitz-Birkenau as well as several death marches before arriving at Dachau. After being finally released, he arrived in France in February 1946, where he was reunited with a brother and a sister. He didn't share with them anything about what he had endured, just as he never spoke about it with his three children later on.

It wasn't until 1985, forty years after the end of the war, with the release of the movie Shoah, that he finally opened up. For two years, whenever he had a moment, in the evenings or on weekends, he worked on a manuscript. It tells the story of his life and attempts to explain the workings of the infernal Nazi machine. Nicolas wants the world to understand its sophistication. Nicholas feels his role as a former deportee is to warn people about the depths of humanity's evil potential, so that another Hollocaust nerver happens again.

“And then we walked for days”

-JEANETTE -

(6)

THE DEATH MARCHES

Sarah

On January 18, 1945, after being separated from my mother for two months, I was sent on a death march. We walked for three days, in a half-mile long convoy. We could hear gunshots every so often.

The Nazis had told us,
"If you don't walk, we'll shoot you."

There were bodies scattered all over. Miraculously, on the second day, I found my mother. Then we arrived at Gleivitz. We were put on open coal cars. We traveled like this for five days and five nights, without food or water, except for the third night, when some prisoners came to give us soup at a train station.

Then we arrived at Bergen-Belsen. It was a real deathtrap, ravaged by a typhus epidemic. I caught it too. I had a raging fever, was delirious, with diarrhea and nothing to cover myself, and, of course, not enough time to go to the latrine. My mother took care of me. She would steal hot water from the kitchen and give me spoonfuls of water to fight dehydration; I used to tell her that I would never see Paris again. She would answer, "Nonsense, you will survive." It lasted eight days. With this disease, either you die, or you make it. Thanks to her, I survived; I feel that she gave birth to me twice. When I came out of my delirium, I was very hungry, but there was nothing left to eat in the camp. One rutabaga per day for twenty people. People were on their hands and knees, scratching the dirt to find the smallest piece of grass. There were bodies everywhere, and those bodies were not the peaceful looking ones of people who die in their beds.

"My mother took care of me; I feel that she gave birth to me twice."

- SARAH -

Death march Forced marches of prisoners over long distances, typically during the final months of the war, as the Nazis evacuated camps ahead of advancing Allied forces. Prisoners were often shot if they could not keep up.

"We were forced to march in formation, like soldiers. If your shoes fit, you were lucky. If they didn't, every step was agony. You had to keep walking. There was no other option. I know it sounds ridiculous, but it's true: something as simple as stopping to fix your shoe could mean death."

- LEON -

Judith

We had been marching for four days, we didn't know where we were going, and it didn't seem to matter anymore. The reason for the death march was because The Germans were trying to keep us from being liberated.

I remember walking with a girl named Rosy and her mother. But her mother couldn't go any further and collapsed. The SS shot her mother on the spot, and he just walked away. I'll never forget that moment.

Nissen

It was January in Eastern Europe. The winter was brutal—freezing cold. I had been marching for days. Days. My body had nothing left to give. I couldn't go on. I thought, Maybe I should just step out of line. They'll shoot me, and it will be over. As I made that decision—as I was about to step out—a young man came up to me. Let me tell you, on this death march, no one spoke. No one. So when this man came to talk to me, I was shocked.

He told me he was from Kosice—just like me. And he wouldn't let me give up. "No, no, no, don't do that. I'll help you." I looked at him. "What can you do? You're not in better shape than I am. You're not going to shlep me." But he did. He carried me. Or rather—he dragged me.

He put my hand over his head, and he schlepped me forward. For two, three days.

After those days, my right foot—it was in agony. Frozen solid. Every step was torture.

Then an SS officer came up to me and barked, "Move!" I couldn't walk. I showed him my foot, broken and blue from the cold. He looked at me. On his belt, he had a canteen. Like a small flask. An army bottle. He took it off his belt and handed it to me.

Sweet, hot, black coffee. The SS gave it to me! I couldn't believe it. And believe me when I say—when I drank that coffee, I felt like I was being resurrected. Revived. I could feel it moving through me. Warming my veins. My organs. I became stronger. I walked again.

Then, we came to a steep mountain, like in Germany. The temperature was sub-freezing. My ears—I couldn't feel them. It was like they had turned to ice. I was afraid that if I touched them, they would break off.

I turned to him showing my ears... they're freezing. He looked at me, took off his SS cap, placed it on my head, pulled it down over my ears.

And I never saw him again.

Death marches.

Robert

Just like in the camp, when we went to work, we had to walk five abreast. We would walk along the road, our arms around each other's shoulders. We walked between 27 and 50 miles in all. Halfway through, we stopped to sleep for a few hours.Some of us lay down in hay inside a barn, while others slept in a brick factory.

The next day, we resumed our march. With the cold, the fatigue, and the hunger, one by one, we began to collapse. But if one of us showed signs of weakening, the others would shake him and get him to continue. At one point, I got really sick, and they walked me to a cart farther up in the convoy. Sitting inside were German prostitutes who worked in the camp for the SS, the kapos, and the officers. The women covered me right away with their fur coats and their covers, and I fell asleep.

It felt like a dream—and more than anything,
it was a true miracle.

Élie

Because of the intense cold, the snow froze on our clothes, which became as brittle as glass. To avoid injury, we had to stay as straight as ice statues. The march lasted 3 days before we finally arrived at Buchenwald.

During the trip, my feet had frozen. They hurt so much during the role calls that I wanted to go to the infirmary. There, the doctor, a deportee from Hungary, told me that my feet would have to be amputated. I refused categorically and managed to run away. When I came back to the block, one of my comrades, a Russian fellow, advised me to soak my feet, alternating between hot and cold water. The other prisoners managed to fill up two tin cans with snow, heating one of them on the stove in our barrack. By doing this, the condition of my feet quickly improved.

Élie Buzyn suffered severe frostbite on his feet during the death marches and later became an orthopedic surgeon.

David Schaecter

David Schaecter was born and raised in Czechoslovakia. In 1940, his father was arrested and sent to a labor camp. A year later, when David was just thirteen, Slovak Hlinka Guards—neighbors he once knew—stormed the family home and drove them out at gunpoint.

He was deported by cattle car—eighty people to a wagon, two buckets for eighty souls. The journey to Auschwitz was suffocating; by the time the doors opened, a quarter of those inside were dead or dying.

On arrival, soldiers separated the deportees. David's mother and his two little sisters were driven toward open pits. Gunfire followed. He was 13 years old.

In the camp, David was assigned to hard labor on the train cars—cleaning wheels and axles, hauling heavy grease canisters as transports kept arriving "filled with more and more people every day." His older brother Jacobo stayed close to him at first, helping him survive—lifting him onto the ramp to be sent to work, sharing what little strength he had left. When the camp water was poisoned, Jacobo was among those who died. David never recovered from that loss. His brother had carried him through those first days, and for the rest of his life, he carried Jacobo within him.

When the war ended, he was fifteen, weighed eighty-three pounds, and was the only survivor among one hundred and five family members. He spent the following years in an orphanage in Prague before beginning to rebuild his life.

Though he has shared his story for decades—speaking to students and communities every week—the wound has never healed. When I sat with him for eight hours, the longest interview in The Last Ones series—out of more than a hundred we've filmed—I understood that even after a lifetime of testimony, telling the story still meant reopening the pain. Bearing witness, for David, remains an act of courage.

Leon Schagrin

Leon Schagrin was born in 1926 in Grybów, Poland. During the liquidation of his community and the Tarnów ghetto, he was forced to work for the killers—driving them from site to site—and witnessed countless shootings, including the murder of his own cousin holding her two children.

In 1941, Leon was captured and sent through a series of ghettos and camps. In 1942, his parents, four sisters, and brother were murdered at the Bełżec extermination camp—a fate he narrowly escaped.

Deported to Auschwitz, he survived the first selection by claiming he worked with horses. Inside the camp, he was stripped, shaved, uniformed, and tattooed with the number 161744—a mark that would follow him long after liberation. Later, he was transferred to Auschwitz III (Buna) for industrial labor, where he remained through the brutal winter evacuations until liberation.

After the war, Leon's struggle continued. Years later, unable to bear looking at the number tattooed on his arm, he covered it with a panther. It was his way of reclaiming his body, his name, and his story — an act of taking back what Auschwitz had tried to erase.

But even that could not undo the damage within. The trauma was too deep. Leon could never bring himself to have children — because the shadow of what he had lived through left no space for new life.

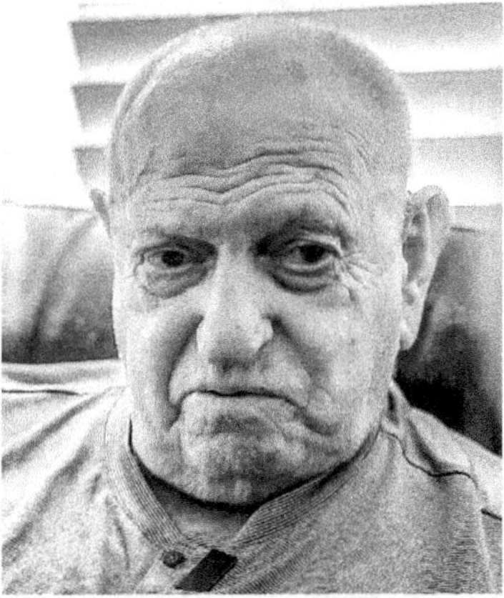

Esther Senot

Born in Poland in 1928, Esther grew up in the Belleville neighborhood of Paris, where her parents moved to in 1930. She lived happily with her six brothers and sisters, until everything changed on July 16, 1942, the day of the Vel' d'Hiv' round-up. At her mother's request, Esther went to see what was going on in the neighborhood. Because she wasn't home at the time, she avoided getting arrested. But when she returned to her house, she found the apartment empty, and the door sealed.

Alone in Paris at the age of 14, with nothing but a little summer dress on her back, she was first taken in by a building attendant whom she knew before finding refuge with one of her brothers in Pau (southwest of France). She eventually returned to Paris in the hope of finding her parents. But she was in turn arrested and taken to Auschwitz in a particularly dreadful convoy made up of old people arrested at a retirement home and women with their newborn babies.

Esther is one of the few deportees I've met who lasted two winters in Auschwitz-Birkenau. Upon her return, like most Jewish survivors, she found herself in Paris, at the Hotel Lutetia, which served as an assembly point, but no one came to pick her up because no one in her family had come back. She returned to Belleville to see what had become of her family's apartment, which she was told she could get back, if she paid back all the unpaid rent.

Totally destitute, she found no help anywhere; she even had the feeling of "disturbing" a country determined to live again.

On the rare occasions she would try to talk about what she had endured; she would feel people didn't believe her. So, she kept quiet. She tried to take her own life, but she survived and, a few months later, met the man who was to become her husband. Together, they have three children, six grandchildren and as many great-grandchildren. The young girl who became an orphan at the age of 14 took revenge on life with her family.

(7)

THE END OF THE WAR

Henri

By the end of the war, I had landed in yet another camp. I managed to escape with a friend, and in a nearby village, we stumbled upon a group of American soldiers. We ran to them, crying, trying to tell them our story. But how could they believe us? What we'd lived through wasn't even believable. We somehow convinced them to come and see the camp for themselves. They took us in their jeep. They saw the bodies on the Appelplatz. The odor was sickening. There were decaying bodies everywhere. The trucks no longer came to pick them up to cremate them. We didn't know it then, but it was the very first time American soldiers had entered a concentration camp. They immediately alerted the general staff: Eisenhower, Bradley, and Patton came on April 12, 1945.

There, in the camp, General Eisenhower, Supreme Allied Commander, said, "Our boys now know why they are fighting." It meant that all those who had obstinately stood in the way would finally see the reality. We later understood our small role in being the first to show them these unimaginable things.

The discovery of the Ohrdruf camp by the Americans.

Élie

In Buchenwald, in 1945, when the Americans learned what we had gone through, they tried to give us weapons so we could take revenge. In front of trucks filled with German prisoners, they handed us machine guns and said: "Go ahead, shoot! It doesn't matter." None of us did it; we didn't want to become killers like them. We were thinking: you wanted to exterminate us, it didn't work, we are going to go on living.

That will be our revenge.

Buchenwald camp.

"We didn't want to become killers like them."

- ÉLIE -

"48 more hours and I would have died. I know what it is to feel yourself dying"

- FLORA -

Flora

When the soldiers entered the camp, I was in Bergen Belsen, they recoiled at what they saw: we were like zombies. I had been very lucky to survive. 48 more hours and I would have died. I know what it is to feel yourself dying. At one point, I felt completely at peace, even happy. I smiled, detached from everything around me. In my daze, I remember seeing a pretty young girl getting up, falling and dying.

Then, I ended up in a camp for prisoners, where we were given cards to write to our families. We were supposed to tell them we were alive, but without telling them what had happened to us. Our words were already censored.

David

I was still in the hands of the SS, locked in that train, with no idea where we were going—when suddenly, the American Air Force bombed it. I don't know how, but I managed to jump out. I ran into the forest, my heart pounding. I stayed there, hiding for more than eight days. I was starving, freezing, and terrified.

Then I was spotted by a soldier—a Czech. He didn't turn me in. He helped me. He picked me up and carried me to a field hospital.

When the war finally ended, I was 15 years old and weighed only 83 pounds. Out of 105 members of my family, I was the only one left. I was placed in an orphanage in Prague, where I stayed until I was 20.

Judith

One morning, I woke up outdoors, exhausted and weak. I opened my eyes—and for once, they weren't SS. They were Russian soldiers. My first sight of freedom wasn't the joyful liberation I had imagined. I saw them dragging someone behind a barn and shooting him. That was my first sight of freedom—death, again. It wasn't the joyful liberation I had imagined. I had this vision that when we would be liberated there would be chocolate and flowers, dancing and hugging!

But that wasn't the case for me.

Élie

At the end of the war, the Americans liberated us from Buchenwald and housed us in concrete SS barracks outside the camp. There were showers, toilets, and we had our own beds; we had lots to eat, but we were still stuck there.

General de Gaulle's niece, who had been deported to Ravensbrück as a resistance fighter, learned that, at Buchenwald, there was a group of orphaned young people who refused to return to Eastern Europe, where their families had been murdered, and therefore had nowhere to go. Very upset by this situation, she talked to her uncle, who decided that France would welcome 423 of these 900 minors and make them wards of the state. In other words, France would adopt them. Switzerland would take the sick, while the others would be dispatched throughout Western Europe, including Sweden. This is how we learned that we would leave the camp to go somewhere in Europe.

We left Germany in rotting train cars. When we reached the French border, we travelled first class and were greeted with sweets and marching bands, but it was all propaganda for the media. When we arrived, we were quarantined in a house in Calvados. We were not happy to be locked up again after surviving the camps.

Robert

On May 8, 1945, I was told that the war had ended. It was also my fifteenth birthday. I don't know if that was the reason, but I burst into tears. I cried and cried and cried. I couldn't stop crying. Two of my friends scolded me: "The war is over and you're crying!" But I couldn't help it. I leaned, limp, against a wall and didn't move any more.

When I was taken from the camp, I was the same height I am now, five feet two, and I weighed 35 pounds, a real skeleton. I haven't grown any taller since.

Because of my poor health, I was evacuated by plane. At the Bichat Hospital, I was alone in a room, hooked up to several IVs. I was lifeless; my eyes were closed. I didn't speak, even to my mother who visited me every day. One day, she came into my room, room 15, and she saw that my bed had been made. She thought I had died during the night. She ran to see the doctors who told her that I was alive and that they had decided to give me electroshock therapy. That's when I said to my mother: "I don't want electroshocks. I want you to get me out of this hospital." Those were my first words !

At the Liberation, around one thousand underage survivors were found in Buchenwald. After long negotiations, 426 of these children were repatriated to France and taken in by the OSE — the Children's Aid Society. Léon Lewkowicz and Élie Buzyn were among them.

Léon Lewkowicz (1)

Élie Buzyn (2)

LVT

“When I arrived at
the Lutetia Hotel,
I weighed 62 pounds”

- GINETTE -

Ginette [2]

When I arrived at the Lutetia Hotel, I weighed 62 pounds. Like many others, I couldn't sleep in a bed—I had to sleep on the floor. There were around 200 of us, and they gave us food in two meal services. Some people lined up twice, they were so hungry.

But you know, many died because they ate too much, too fast. I couldn't eat at all. I had dysentery, I was bleeding. I spent two months in the hospital. Every day, they gave me a tiny spoonful of raw minced horse meat. We had to re-learn how to eat.

Sarah

After the war, family members, thinking they were doing the right thing, fed us loads of food and we would end up throwing up. Also, we couldn't sleep in a bed anymore. So, for several months, as soon as we were alone in our room, we would lock the door and sleep on the floor.

Flora

When we got to the Lutetia Hotel, we were infested with lice. I stayed there 8 days. We slept on the floor, as we could no longer sleep in a bed. When we were given bread, we would hide it, keeping it, just in case. I remember that they filmed our bodies, especially our chests, because we no longer had any breasts at all. I was given a pair of underwear, a slip, a shirt, a skirt, a blouse, tights, shoes, a few francs, and that was it.

Lutetia In 1945, the very chic Parisian hotel Lutetia — headquarters of the Nazis during the Occupation — was transformed for several months into a reception center for many survivors of the Nazi concentration camps. Eighteen thousand repatriates passed through its doors.

Delousing, disinfection, medical examinations. The weakest were sent to hospitals. Those strong enough, and who still had family or somewhere to go, left the hotel. Others stayed there for weeks.

"I didn't recognize her. She had yellowish skin, protruding cheekbones, and teary eyes. My mother didn't recognize me either."

Esther

When we were repatriated to the Hotel Lutetia, we saw hundreds of people who were waiting with pictures of their loved ones in their hands, photos taken before the war, where they looked healthy and well. You can imagine that even if we had seen them, we wouldn't have been able to recognize them. The luckiest ones had found their families and managed to go home with a metro ticket and a little bit of money.

Nobody came to look for me.

My entire family had been arrested and deported. Out of my six brothers and sisters, I had only one brother left, who was in the army. I had nothing left and nowhere to go. I was 17 years old and, since I was a minor, I wasn't allowed to leave. So, I stayed at the Lutetia almost until they closed it.

Yvette

When I arrived at the Hotel Lutetia, I didn't know if my parents were still alive. I sent them a message by pneumatic mail, as we didn't have a phone at home. Mommy was doing the dishes. She dropped everything and ran. She came wearing her blue apron, her coin purse in one hand and a metro ticket in the other. It's an image I'll never forget.

At the hotel, she asked where I was. An employee called me on the loudspeaker: "Miss Dreyfus is requested at the front desk." I went there and saw a lady with white hair.

I didn't recognize her. She had yellowish skin skin, protruding cheekbones, and teary eyes. My mother didn't recognize me either.

We had not seen each other for a year, and I weighed barely 79 pounds. We looked at each other for a while, then I cried, "Mommy!" We fell into each other's arms, crying, and she said, "Let's go." We were not given money for a cab or anything, so we took the metro. At home, my father was in tears. He was a tall and handsome man. He was sitting on a chair, staring at me, trying to figure out if it was really me.

I never told them anything about the camps.
They were sad enough.

Lucette

Upon arriving at Hotel Lutetia, I refused to go in. Somebody had told me that my mother was alive in Bichat Hospital, but I didn't believe them. At the selection, I had seen her being sent to the opposite side. It was sure it must be a mistake. Maybe it was someone else with the same name. I had to know. At first, the police refused to let me leave. They told me I wasn't allowed, but I told them I was allowing myself. So, I went straight to the hospital without stopping at the Lutetia. In the hospital corridor, a supervisor said to me, "You must be Lucette. I'm going to speak to your mother, then come back for you."

When I saw my mom, I got the shock of my life.

First of all, I didn't recognize her. I had recovered a little, but my mom, who used to be so beautiful, was a skeleton. The doctors did all they could, but it wasn't much. She had serious heart problems. She spent the rest of her life in and out of hospitals, just managing to survive.

Lucette with her mother — both survived the camps,
but her mother never recovered.

Judith Sherman

Judith H. Sherman was born in 1931 in the village of Kurima, Slovakia. Her childhood ended with the outbreak of World War II, when antisemitic decrees, displacement, and fear reshaped daily life.

In 1944, she was arrested and deported to Auschwitz. The transport, she recalled, was a nightmare — crammed into a cattle wagon with no room to sit, one bucket in the middle that quickly overflowed, no water for days, the air so thick and unbearable that people began to lose their minds from thirst. At one point, a desperate man forced his way through a small window and jumped.

Upon arrival, she narrowly escaped the gas chambers when her wagon was sent back out due to overcrowding. She was later transferred to Ravensbrück, where she endured selections, brutality, and constant hunger. In 1945, during a death march, she was liberated by Russian soldiers.

After the war, Judith returned to a homeland emptied of Jewish life and family. Seeking a new beginning, she emigrated first to England and then to the United States, where she rebuilt her life and became a social worker and psychotherapist.

The war never fully left her. Even decades later, she described small, lasting habits — like refusing to "select" fruit at the supermarket, always taking whatever was on top — and she never wore striped clothing again. The memories of the camps had etched themselves into her daily life.

Jeanette Spiegel

Jeanette was born in Vienna in 1923 and grew up there with her sister, Irma. During Kristallnacht, her family's fabric shop—half wood, half glass—stayed dark and silent after a warning to keep the door shut; the children were told not to go near it. Soon after, her parents sent her to an aunt in Belgium for safety.

At sixteen in Brussels, she repeatedly slipped past the Gestapo—once by asking to take her kitten downstairs, then jumping onto a crowded trolley as strangers urged the driver not to stop. On April 1 she was denounced, arrested, and deported to Auschwitz, where she was tattooed and assigned to the Kanada Commando, bundling coats and sorting stolen belongings. She found small ways to resist: damaging good garments so they wouldn't be reused and disposing of jewelry so the Nazis wouldn't profit. Food was meager—a scrap of bread, a dab of margarine, thin soup.

When the camp emptied, she layered blouse, sweater, and jacket despite orders, slipped away during the death march, and, with fluent German and fair features, passed as non-Jewish to reach safety. After the war she learned her parents and sister were gone. A cousin helped her immigrate to the United States.

Jeanette confided to me that, after the war, she hoped to marry a man who could offer her stability — a way to quiet the fear of ever going without again. Even today, she keeps a few pieces of jewelry on her at all times, "just enough to escape if I ever have to."

At 101, she wears around her neck a necklace engraved with the names of her descendants — a reminder that from all she lost came generations who live because she survived.

Jean Vaislic

Jean was born in Lodz, Poland, in 1926. He was thirteen when the German army entered his home town. The following year, when his father was arrested, Jean managed to escape. He hid from farm to farm before being arrested and deported to Auschwitz in 1942. He was 16 years old.

Liberated at 20, he was the only survivor of a family that numbered around sixty before the war. For him, returning to Poland was out of the question, as the emptiness that awaited him would lead to suicide. Not knowing where to go, he follows Vincent, a Polish friend he met during the deportation, who has taken him under his wing and whom he considers a brother.

They go to Toulouse, where Jean wanders the streets for a while without finding any help. There he also met Marie, another former deportee, who was to become his wife. Marie was arrested at the age of 14, on denunciation, and sent to Ravensbrück in August 1944. She survived the death marches that took her to Bergen-Belsen, which had become a veritable hospital where a typhus epidemic decimated the survivors and from which she narrowly escaped. On her return to Toulouse, she was lucky enough to find her family.

Jean couldn't imagine having children; he didn't want anyone to know that he had been deported, or even that he was Jewish. It was out of love for Marie that he finally changed his mind. Together, they had two sons. Until very recently, no one knew that John and Mary were a couple of former deportees. Even today, when Jean recalls his memories, it's "as if someone was shooting at him", he says, pale.

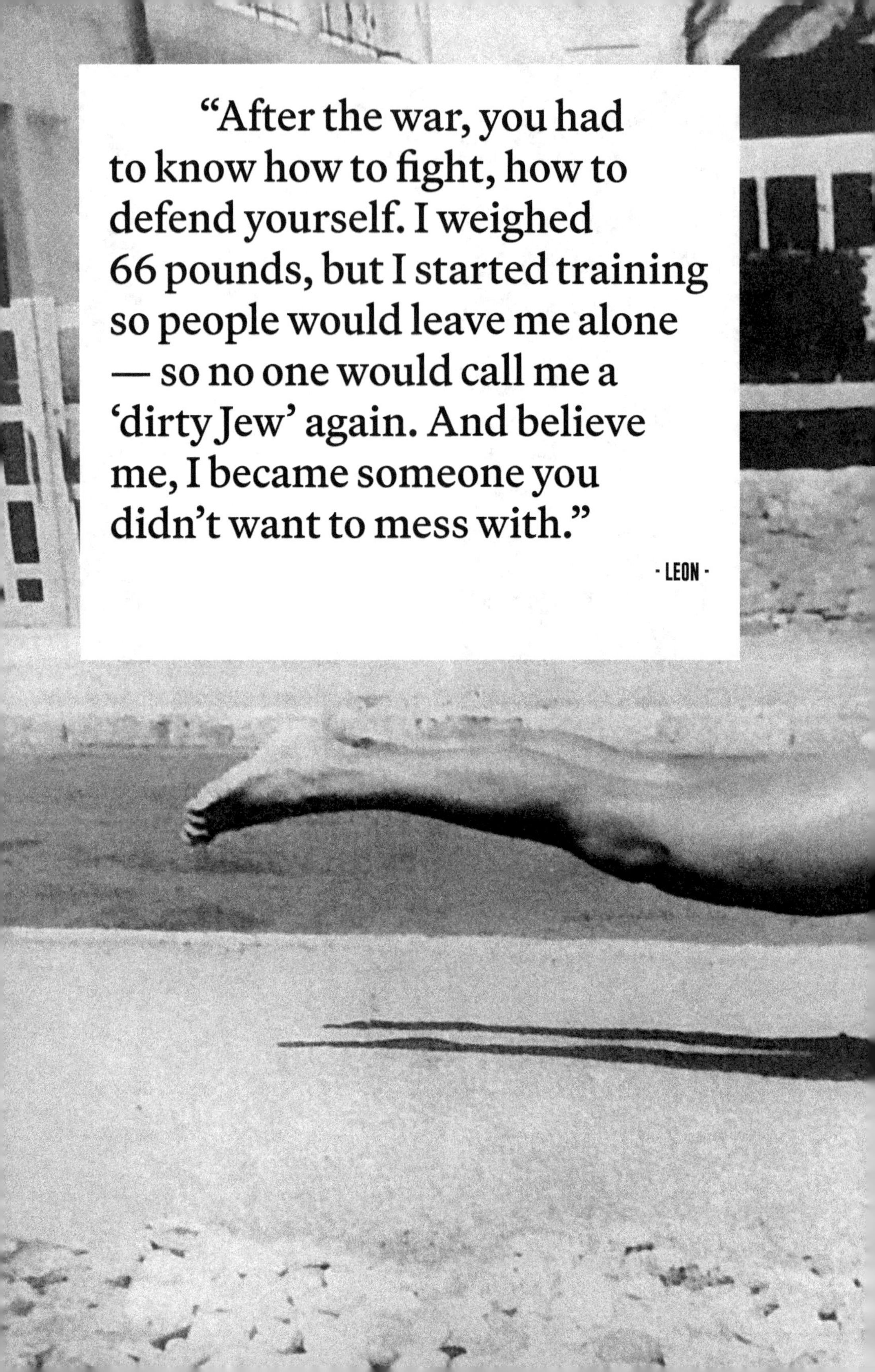

"After the war, you had to know how to fight, how to defend yourself. I weighed 66 pounds, but I started training so people would leave me alone — so no one would call me a 'dirty Jew' again. And believe me, I became someone you didn't want to mess with."

- LEON -

(8)

THE WEIGHT OF AUSCHWITZ

Esther

I had to leave the Lutetia... it was closing. But I was alone. At just 17 years old, I wandered the streets of Paris by myself. I needed to find a job, but in my physical and psychological state, it wasn't easy—especially since I had no formal training. Then I got fed up with it since I couldn't find a solution, so I tried to commit suicide. I ended up in a psychiatric hospital. From time to time, I would emerge from my torpor and then go back to sleep. In moments of clarity, I told myself that I couldn't possibly end my life like that.

Then, little by little, I came back to life. I found a small room and a job as a salesperson. You know, I was so lonely. At the time, there was no psychological help. it wasn't easy to rebuild your life on your own. I started to live a fairly normal life, then a coworker asked me to go on vacation with her. It was a first for me!

In the house next door lived a young man
who became my husband.

Jeanette

The war was over, but I felt no relief. I had escaped, but I wasn't free. The city I grew up in was different. Or maybe I was different. The streets I had walked as a child, the buildings I once knew—they were still there, but they didn't feel the same. Vienna wasn't my home anymore. I didn't have a home. And I was about to learn that there was nothing left to go back to.

I went to every organization, every list, every agency. I searched for my family. My mother, my father, my sister. I had little hope but maybe one of them had survived? Maybe I wasn't alone?

One by one, the names of the dead came back to me. My parents. My sister. My aunts, my uncles. The people I loved—gone.

I was alone.
I had survived, but for what?
What does survival mean when there is no one left?

I had spent so long just trying to live one more day, one more hour, one more step. And now, I had to figure out how to keep living. But how do you rebuild when there is nothing left?

"I couldn't find any solution, so I tried to commit suicide"

- ESTHER -

Jean and his wife Marie.

Jean

After the war, I had no one left — I was the only survivor out of sixty members of my family. There wasn't much of a choice—Either you gave up and ended it, or you tried to live like a man. So I took matters into my own hands and started from nothing. I worked as a boilermaker for three or four years, until I found something a little less backbreaking. But the most important thing? In 1950, I met Marie. We got married a year later.

I didn't want any children. If it hadn't been for the love of my wife, I wouldn't have had any. I had a visceral fear that everything would happen again. I was thinking that if today's civilization, in the century we are living in, allowed thugs to do such things, there was no reason it wouldn't happen again. This fear was gnawing at me so much that I even kept my fake name.

I'm grateful I met my wife and had three children. Without them, I don't know what would have become of me. It's the greatest reward God could give me...

And look at me now, I'm talking like an old fool!

"Either you gave up and ended it, or you tried to live like a man"

- JEAN -

A marriage in Robert's family, before the war.

Élie

After the war, I had nothing—no family, no one. So I went to Paris and started studying medicine. And the man whose feet had frozen during the death march between Auschwitz and Buchenwald became an orthopedic surgeon.

I was single for a very long time; I spent my time studying and working. Then, one day, a young woman was brought to the hospital after a car accident. I spent all night operating, trying to save her legs. She said to one of her friends who came to visit her, "Go see the surgeon, he has beautiful eyes." For her friend and I, it was love at first sight. We stayed together from that day on. We got married and had three children.

Ginette and her husband.

Jacques and Lucie Altmann and their daughter Sylvie.

"I think I left my feelings at the camp."

- GINETTE -

Ginette [1]

When I arrived at home, in the apartment I still live in today, it was my mother who opened the door. I no longer felt any emotions. I was numb. So, when my mother told me that she was waiting to hear from Daddy and Gilbert, my little brother, I could only snap, "you won't hear from them. Daddy and Gilbert were gassed and their bodies have been burned." I don't even know if she realized what "gassed" meant but it must have been terrible for her when I said that their bodies had been burned. But at the time, I didn't know what I was saying. The remorse came later. I know now that my feelings had stayed at the camp.

Crying is something I can't do anymore;
it's terrible to say,
but nothing brings tears in my eyes anymore.

I didn't get married right away. I met my future husband in 1952, and we got married three months later. We wanted to have a child. My son was born eight years after the end of the war; it was better that way. Those who had children right after the war encountered health problems. Their bodies couldn't keep up; they had been too severely damaged.

One child was enough for us: we were never home. We used to leave the house early in the morning to work in the street market. Besides, I've never been a nurturing mother.

I think I left my feelings at the camp. Since then, I've never been able to cry. Recently, while listening to some young girls read a passage, I could almost feel the tears well up in my eyes. I said to myself: "There, I'm feeling something again, that's good."

Flora

Sometimes, people tell me I'm peculiar because I never cry. Since the camp, I can no longer cry, even at funerals. I'm beginning to believe that I was desensitized by the camp.

Esther

For years, I had this recurring **nightmare**: I saw myself arriving at the camp, on the ramp, with two of my children. I wondered how I was going to manage, knowing all too well that it was impossible to get out of Auschwitz alive with two children. Of course, I would awake with a start.

Sarah

For a very long time, even after I was married, I would have **nightmares**. It was always about the camp. At night, I would scream in my sleep. My husband would shake me up, hold me in his arms and kiss me. It's funny, because since he passed away, about twenty years ago, I don't have nightmares anymore. It's as if it stopped because I didn't have anyone whose arms I could cry in.

Jacques

At night, in my **nightmares**, I would try to strangle my wife. I would dream that someone wanted to steal my piece of bread, so I would grab my wife by the neck and squeeze her very tightly as if to defend myself. It went on for several years, and I finally had to see a psychiatrist to stop it.

“I would try to strangle my wife.”

- JACQUES -

Ginette [2]

We were supposed to go back to a normal life, to move on. But it stays with you, always lurking in the corner of your mind.

You know, sometimes at night, I'm back in Auschwitz. And when I wake up in the morning, my bed is a battlefield. No one can ever truly understand what we endured. No one. We didn't talk about it. We couldn't. And then, when we finally did, people dismissed us.

"The deportees are crazy" they said. "They're making things up", but we weren't. We were telling the truth. The problem was, our truth was just... unfathomable.

Élie

We wanted to resume a normal life, both at work and at home. That's why I didn't speak up. At home, only my wife, Etty, knew everything. At night, I had nightmares. I would wake up startled as if I had been called for the Appelplatz or something else. It went on for a very long time.

I felt like there was an enormous pit behind me that had swallowed up all my relatives, along with millions of others.

They were in that pit, just behind me. At the age of 17 or 18, I had an acute sense that if I looked behind me into the pit, I would end up jumping into it as well. I felt an imminent danger of suicide. Therefore, just like a horse who is made to wear blinders, I forced myself to never look back or even to the side to look only straight ahead.

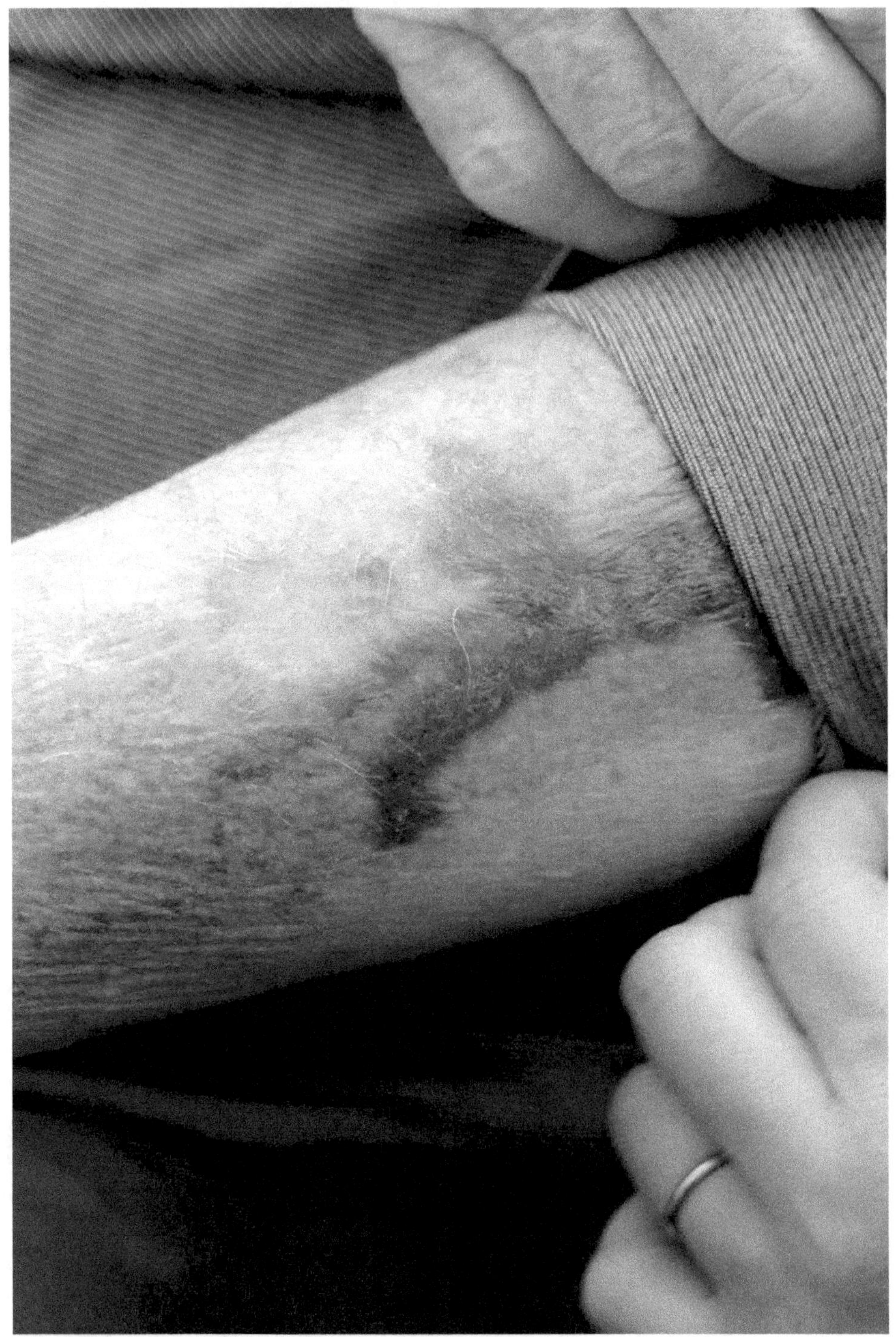

“I couldn’t stand seeing the number so had a panther tattoed over it”

Leon and his wife Betty on their wedding day — both survivors of the camps. They never wanted to have children.

Leon

The horrors I witnessed and endured—they've stayed with me all my life, just like the number tattooed on my arm: 161744.

I couldn't look at it anymore. Every time I saw those numbers, I was back there. I didn't want to carry history on my skin forever, so I covered it. I had a panther tattooed over the number—strong and fierce, a symbol of survival. It felt like reclaiming something, a way to rewrite part of the story.

The damage ran so deep that I knew I could never be a father. The idea of raising children—I couldn't do it. The trauma had taken too much from me.

Ginette [1]

I never throw anything away. I always finish my plate — I eat everything, even when it's expired. And even at a restaurant, I can't stand seeing someone leave a piece of bread.

Judith

You can't leave it behind—it won't let you. The trauma stays with you, shaping the smallest, most unexpected parts of your life.

For instance, I never wear stripes. Ever. They remind me too much of the pajamas, the ones we were forced to wear. It's irrational, maybe, but it's real.

And when I go to the supermarket, I don't pick through the fruit, searching for the best ones like everyone else. I just take whatever is on top. Because of Mengele. Because of the selections. I can't bring myself to make a choice like that.

I have these habits, these reflexes, and most people wouldn't understand. But they are part of me now, memories of a time that never really let me go.

“I’ve got my shtiks, my quirks...
I never wear stripes”

- JUDITH -

Albert Veissid

Albert was born in Constantinople, Turkey, in 1924. He was just eight months old when his family moved to Lyon, France. Then, his brother was born. As a teenager, he worked as a salesman in a fabric store and attended the music conservatory, where he studied guitar and clarinet.

Arrested at work, he was taken to Drancy, where he made friends with the person in charge of the garbage bins, who would use them to pass on messages and objects. That's how he managed to send a letter to his parents, telling them to hide; it would save them.

Deported to Auschwitz on convoy 75, he pretended to be a bricklayer, and was selected to work in a building outside the camp, alongside Poles. The Nazis decided to look for musicians among the Jewish inmates to form an orchestra, and Albert successfully auditioned. Albert was now the clarinet player for the Auschwitz orchestra. They played in the mornings, when the deportees left for work, and in the evenings, when they would return to the camp. The rest of the day, the musicians would rehearse in a room located under the Auschwitz brothel, which was another one of the "entertainments" the Nazis enjoyed, as well as Sunday family concerts.

Albert narrowly survived the death marches. After the war, he was diagnosed with a collapsed lung. He would lose a lung and never played the clarinet again. He nevertheless continued his musical career, playing the guitar.

In 2009, while renovation was taking place in a building in the Auschwitz camp, a glass bottle containing a message was found in a wall. On the message were inscribed the names of seven deportees: six Polish Christians and one French Jew - Albert Veissid.

For Albert, who had no recollection of the existence of this genuine "bottle in the sea", launched at the time by the prisoners in the hope that they would not be forgotten, it was the greatest surprise of his life. Albert died in 2019, just two months after sharing his story with Les Derniers/The Last Ones.

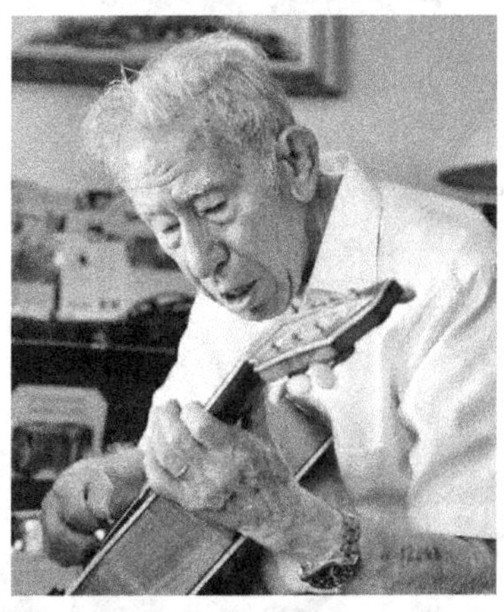

Robert Wajcman

Robert was born in France on 8 May 1930 to a father who was an antique dealer at a flea market. In 1944, he was shot, and he and his mother were taken to Drancy, then deported to Auschwitz on the penultimate convoy.

He was 14, but pretended to be 16, which enabled him to avoid being sent directly to the gas chamber, like around half of his convoy, i.e. around 500 people. Separated from his mother, he knew nothing of his fate. In the winter of 1945, he made the "death marches" to Buchenwald.

On his 15th birthday, he learned that he had been liberated and began to cry his eyes out, having held them back for months. He weighed only 16 kilos and remained prostrate, unable to move. Repatriated to Paris by plane, he was hospitalised at the Hôpital Bichat in a very worrying condition. His mother, who also survived, visited him every day, but he didn't even have the strength to talk to her. After several months, she was finally able to take him home. Robert regained his human form and began studying art, but soon stopped to help his mother at the flea market, where she had taken over her husband's stall.

They were badly received by some antique dealers, who regretted the flourishing business they had done during the war and resented having to return to their rightful owners the shops they had appropriated while in hiding or in the camps.

For a long time, Robert kept silent. He decided to testify when he heard the first Holocaust deniers claim that the gas chambers were designed to kill lice. Testifying remains an ordeal for him, but his concern for the future drives him to do so.

(9)

TO SPEAK OR TO STAY SILENT

Sarah during a visit to Auschwitz.

Jacques

After the war, when we tried to speak about it, even just a little, people refused to believe us. They used to say, "Here come the meshugge." In their eyes, that's all we were, "meshugge," which means crazy in Yiddish. When we talked about the gas chambers and the horrors we had witnessed at the ramp, nobody believed us.

Sarah

When I came back, I wasn't allowed to talk about it, even with family members. My aunts and uncles would tell me to forget about it. As if you could forget that.

I returned to Auschwitz after fifty-three years with my son and daughter. When I saw the train tracks and ruins, I suddenly felt that I no longer feared death. Who knows how it will be? In a daze, I said to myself that I could now share with people and talk about it. Since that day, I haven't stopped talking about it.

"You don't live after Auschwitz — you live with it, until you die."

- SARAH -

Jean

At first, I wanted to forget. I tried to bury all those memories deep within me. Why did fate want me to live? I don't know. My whole family was dead. I ended up all alone at the end of the war. Today, when the memories come back to me, it still feels like I'm being shot at. As soon as my memories resurface, I become pale, I feel like I'm being strangled. Even at my age, it makes me sick as a dog, if you'll excuse the expression. My memories choke me.

I'm 92, and I still haven't processed it. I should know how to swim by now, but as far as I'm concerned, you never can get your head above water.

"When the memories come back to me, it feels like I'm being shot at."

- JEAN -

Flora

I didn't talk about it for thirty years. When I went back to Marseille, eight months after the end of the war, no one expected to see me return. I felt out of place. I managed practically all on my own and said nothing.

Later, when I started telling my story, people would tell me, "Stop, you're making me sick."

Some of my friends bragged about not having been arrested. They told me: "But why did you let them arrest you?" I answered, "But the person who came to arrest me was French, really French, not German. How could I have known what was going to happen?"

For the past ten years or so, now that I'm reaching the end of my life, I think about it more often than ever. But when I talk about it, I'm told, that's enough, it's in the past, just forget it. But the people who tell me that lived with their mothers, their parents, all their lives. For those of us who have lost everything, how can we forget?

I share my story, but it makes me sick. The last time, my blood pressure went way up. I promised my daughter that I wouldn't talk about it anymore. She doesn't know that I'm talking to you today. Before I leave this earth, I wanted to talk one more time, so the young people know about it.

Élie

I was one of those who would tell his fellow deportees not to tell children about what we had gone through.

One day, my best friend Armand — whom I met in Buchenwald and who has a daughter — asked me; "If your daughter asks where your parents are, what do you tell her? "I answered, "You avoid it, you say whatever you want, but you don't tell her. Because if you sit your daughter on your lap and you describe the gas chambers and the crematorium where her grandparents were, you are going to destroy her instead of helping her. Telling this to our children, especially when they are young, is like passing our suffering on to them. It's like taking what you have endured for four or five years, putting it in a syringe, and injecting it into your daughter or son intravenously. It's extremely cruel."

That's why I never spoke about it with my children when they were young.

With my grandchildren, it's different. Time has passed, and there's a whole generation between us. So when one of my grandsons came to ask me questions, I decided to take him to Auschwitz and tell him my story. I did the same with my other grandchildren once they reached the age I was — fifteen.

Elie and Armand, his best friend from Buchenwald — both left without family after the war, they stayed as close as brothers for the rest of their lives.

Elie and his grandchildren.

Nissen

I did not just survive. I thrived!

I went back to Auschwitz to celebrate my 90th birthday, with almost my entire family—my wife, my children, my grandchildren, my great-grandchildren.

We were 100. And still, some were missing.

We took a photograph—one that will never be forgotten—standing on the train tracks, the very same tracks where one million Jews were brought to Auschwitz. What a revenge!

Exactly where the cattle cars arrived, where we had once been crammed together, we stood again. But this time, as free people.

We squeezed together—to immortalize the moment. I showed them the cattle coach, and then we started singing.

Nissen with his wife, children, grandchildren and great-grandchildren at Auschwitz.

“My very large family is my revenge.”

- NISSEN -

Nicolas

For a very long time, I didn't share much with my family, because I didn't want to traumatize them. In 1985, I had the idea of taking my daughter to see Lanzmann's movie, Shoah. As we left the movie theater, my daughter asked me, "But Daddy, you were deported, why don't you write your own story?" I replied, "You're right, why not."

At the time, I was working, so I would write only on weekends and during vacation. I wanted to tell what had happened to me but also to talk in detail about the workings of the complex Nazi machine. It took me two or three years. The person who typed the manuscript for me kept asking me for more chapters, as if we were writing a suspense novel.

I'm surprised I have been able to write all that.

Nicolas showing us the manuscript of his book, written with great patience.

> "But Daddy, you were deported, why don't you write your own story?"
>
> - NICOLAS -

Julia and her husband Marcel — along with their baby — both former deportees and war orphans.

"I don't know how they found out that two Holocaust survivors were living there"

- JULIA -

Julia

One day, about thirty years ago, when I had not yet told my story yet, someone knocked at my door. They were two journalists. I was with my husband. I don't know how they found out that two Holocaust survivors were living there, but they asked us if we wanted to share our stories. I said yes. I sat down, and as soon as I started talking, I collapsed. I cried and cried, so much that I couldn't talk. They ended up leaving, but when they came back a few days later, I was finally able to tell them my story.

Esther

In Auschwitz, shortly before her death, I promised my sister Fanny that I would tell what had happened to us. For years, I didn't. Then, in 1985, when I retired, I took a trip to Poland with my husband—supposedly unrelated to my past. During the stay, we were offered an excursion: we could either take a random walk or visit Auschwitz. I thought to myself, I have to go, I've never returned.

At the site, we were guided by a Polish woman who kept talking about the millions of Poles who had been killed. The more I listened, the more I grew angry inside, until I couldn't hold back any longer. I interrupted her "You forget to mention that 98% of them were Jews!" She snapped back at me. She believed I had no right to interrupt her. She thought she knew better than I did! Or at least she thought.

I spent 17 months in Birkenau. Now I am the one who will speak! And that was it—without meaning to, my words poured out, and they haven't stopped since.

Lucette

In the camp, after I was separated from my mother, I cried all the time. People around me were tired of my crying and kept saying, "Lucette, that's enough, you're here for now but, in an hour, you don't know where you're going to be. We need you. You still have a beautiful human face. You are still young. You may have a chance to get out of here alive. For us, it's over." I remember that the people who were saying that were barely thirty years old, only ten years older than I was. "We're counting on you; you will have to tell what happened here." So, you see, mission accomplished. But it's hard, I can't tell you what we went through. How did I survive? I still can't figure it out.

> "It was pushed to such an extreme — anyone who wasn't there couldn't possibly understand what it was like."
>
> - LUCETTE -

Robert

I started speaking up when the Holocaust deniers started saying that the gas chambers were for lice, that the camps were movie sets built by Americans, that it was all nonsense, and none of it had existed.

I speak to young people, aged 14 or 15, the age I was at the time, so they can relate. I receive lots of mail. Some of it has impacted me, specifically a short letter from a kid saying, "I wouldn't have wanted to be in your shoes!" At least he was honest! Another letter read, "In my class, I was one of two Holocaust deniers. After your visit, I'm not one anymore, but my classmate still is."

I'm used to telling my story, but even today, seventy years later, it still makes me feel sick.

Ginette [1]

The first time I told my story was at the end of the 1990s, when Steven Spielberg was filming some deportees. A young man called me to ask if I wanted to tell my story. I told him that I had nothing of interest to say, but he was so insistent that I finally agreed. I talked for three hours.

Later, I reluctantly agreed to go to Auschwitz-Birkenau with a group of young people. I was very afraid that all the memories would flood back. I told myself that I wasn't going to handle it well, that I might even faint. But actually, that was not at all the case. I didn't find anything of what I had lived through over there. To me, Birkenau represented filth, odors, and crowds with people swarming all around, running, screaming, getting hit. Today, that's all gone: everything is clean. What you see is not Birkenau, but something like a movie set.

Since then, I go there with groups, two or three times a year, because if you go there without someone who has lived through it, you don't feel anything. I tell them, "Close your eyes, here, where you just took a step, you can be sure that someone has fallen under the beating of a kapo." I give them little details that bring it to life a bit.

Judith

Despite everything I've been through, people still find it hard to believe when I tell them that luck played the biggest part in my survival. It was the most valuable currency in the camps, and no one can convince me otherwise. Yes, there was strength and resilience, but so much of it came down to being in the right place at the right time. That's why I tell my story. I feel like I owe it to those who weren't as lucky, to the ones who didn't make it.

Ginette [1]

You know, people tend to attribute to me a halo that I don't have, I'm not a heroine. I didn't survive because I was brave what saved me was luck. I left Birkenau in November, which prevented me from being sent to the death march. I was lucky, that's all. I don't know how I survived that. I'd never been very resourceful; I wasn't the kind to get into trouble. But most of all, I didn't have any willpower left. I did whatever I was told without thinking. I just tried to make myself as small as possible, so that nobody would notice me and I wouldn't get hit too often.

Jacques

After the war, I had nothing left. So, I said to myself: "Now, I have to fight. I have to survive to show them that they didn't succeed in exterminating all of us."

So, that's what I did.
I didn't think I could manage, but in the end, I did"

"People tend to attribute to me a halo that I don't have. I'm not a heroine. I didn't survive because I was brave — what saved me was luck."

- GINETTE -

Julia Wallach

Julia was born in Paris in 1925, the only daughter of Polish parents. Her father, a leather craftsman, had his workshop at home, in the apartment she still lives in today and where she welcomed me. Her mother was arrested in July 1942, during the Vel' d'Hiv roundup. She never saw her again.

In April 1943, she was ultimately taken with her father to Drancy, from where she was deported to Auschwitz. She owed her survival in part to one of her cousins, whom she met there, and who advised her never to miss work, under any circumstances, or she too would go "up the chimney". Julia listened to her advice and went to work, even though she was extremely ill with typhus.

In January 1945, the camp was evacuated. Then began the interminable death march, in the freezing cold, which took her to several camps, including Ravensbrück. In April 1945, she managed to escape and, after a long journey, reached American soldiers.

Back in Paris, she managed to recover the family apartment, occupied by a collaborator, and where her father had hidden his modest savings, a few gold coins, in a wall. Thirteen months later, Julia married a former deportee who had returned very ill from the camps, and with whom she led a happy life. She has two children, five grandchildren and six great-grandchildren, with whom she is very close.

Irene Zisblatt

Irene Zisblatt was born in 1929 in the resort town of Polyana, in present-day Ukraine. She grew up in a modest Jewish home until anti-Jewish laws closed in — expelled from school at ten, her world shrinking to fear and isolation.

In April 1944, during Passover, Irene and her family were forced into the Munkács ghetto and soon after deceived into boarding a "work train" bound for Auschwitz. On the way and upon arrival, she recognized familiar faces among the guards—people she had once known—now standing behind the shouts and the guns.

At Auschwitz she was separated from her parents and siblings, becoming the sole survivor among forty relatives. Before selection, her mother had hidden four tiny diamonds in the hem of her skirt—"for bread if you ever escape." Irene kept them by swallowing and recovering them again and again, carrying a small promise through an unthinkable place.

In the camp she was subjected to repeated experiments by Dr. Josef Mengele—painful injections into her eyes, beneath her fingernails, and later a procedure to remove her tattooed number, part of an effort to learn how to erase that ink. The wounds never fully healed.

Near the end of the war, Irene escaped during a death march and was found by American soldiers. Two years later she immigrated to the United States, married, and—despite the experiments meant to deny her that future—had two children.

In time, she chose to speak publicly — and not to just anyone, but to Steven Spielberg! Irene's testimony became part of an Academy Award–winning documentary, making sure the world remembers not numbers, but faces, choices, and the strength behind a single life.

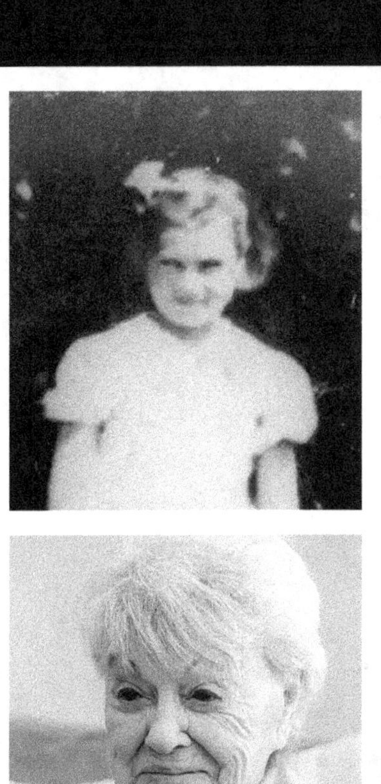

Juif

(10)

NEVER AGAIN?

"I am devastated today when I hear the same rhetoric as in 1940. It's true that History may not repeat itself exactly the same way, but it's strangely similar."

- ESTHER -

Saul

I share my story because the world needs to hear it. Young people need to understand where hatred and intolerance can lead. I never thought I'd see anti-Semitism rear its ugly head again in my lifetime—but here we are. That's why it's more important than ever to remember.

I don't speak for fame or recognition. I speak so that what happened to me, to my family, to millions of others, is not forgotten. I speak so that history does not repeat itself.

It's not easy to relive these memories, but I do it with the hope that it will make a difference. That it will educate, inspire, and move people to take action. Let's learn from the past and build a future with more kindness, more understanding, and more humanity.

Jean & Marie

I said to myself that I never wanted to go through this again. I think that if I had not met my wife, I would have totally erased my Jewishness. If it had been up to me, my children would never have known that they were Jewish.

Marie: Jean even got into an argument with my dad. Jean didn't want our son to be circumcised.

Jean: I was so traumatized by what I had gone through and what I had lost that I said: "No, this shouldn't happen again." I abandoned my religion because of what I had lived through. I have a score to settle with God; perhaps I'll have a word with him when I see him.

Robert

In some schools, when the students find out that the class is about the Holocaust, some of them refuse to attend and leave the classroom. Many schools simply don't ask former deportees to come and talk to the students in order to avoid problems. Do you think it makes us happy to hear comments about Jews on the street? We fear that it could happen again. No matter how often we repeat, "Never again!" there is no guarantee that it will never happen again! I'm worried.

To tell you the truth, I'm very pessimistic.

Lucette

What I see going on in the world now is not good. Antisemitism is still alive. Three years ago, I heard people yelling in my street. I didn't know what was going on, so I opened my window. There was a procession, and it reminded me of when the Germans entered Lyon. If only you knew how much it hurt me!

"You know what they were shouting in the street?
"Death to the Jews!"
It was three years ago.
Nobody said anything or even reacted."

Ginette [1]

I'm convinced that you don't learn anything from history. I've been talking nonstop for the past sixteen years already, and others began long before I did. So, when you see what's going on, with all those radicalized young people, even if they've heard us, it doesn't stop them from being racist or antisemitic. I don't believe my testimony helps. But even though I doubt its usefulness, I am devoting my life to it. Sometimes I speak several times a week, anywhere I am asked. I try to alert young people, to mobilize them against hate. I tell them, "Hate leads to Auschwitz."

Élie

In the face of today's threats, we continue to bury our heads in the sand. To the Islamic State, for example, it's very clear: anyone who is not a radical Islamist must die. In this sense, they are just like the Nazis: they announce their plans, and when they're in a position to carry it out, they go into action. What's bad, is to believe that they will never put their threats into practice, that their words are idle promises. I remember my father's point of view after he had read Mein Kampf. He said: "What Hitler says doesn't matter; he'll never do what he announces."

I was 10, but I still remember it very well.

Nicolas

What matters to me as a former deportee is that no one, whoever they are, should ever have to live through what we did. That's why people today have to know just what people are capable of.

It's clear to me that people don't react enough to the horrors we see every day. What devastates me is that I should have done even more to make things change, to raise awareness. I hope that it will make people think and finally realize that what happened to others can also happen to their children or their grandchildren if they don't react.

Germany
1938

France
2019

David

I remember those mornings, when we were forced to march at six o'clock from the camp to work with the other deportees. People would come out of their homes holding their chamber pots — the containers they used as toilets during the night — and throw the urine and waste at us as we passed. These weren't just ordinary people; they were the intelligentsia, the educated ones, the ones who should have known better. But hate had blinded them.

If it happened then, it can happen now.

Evil doesn't always wear a uniform. Sometimes, it's just the face of a neighbor. Sometimes, it's silence. Sometimes, it's looking the other way.

We have to be careful.
We have to remember.
"Never Again" is not just a promise.
It's a warning.
Because it can happen again.

Anti-Semitic graffiti on the facade of a Paris store and on a mailbox design by C215.

Jeanette

I have told my story for years. To students, to my grandchildren, to anyone who will listen. Because if I don't, who will? If we forget, it will happen again.

And it can happen again.

People think it's history, something far away. But I remember how it started. It didn't begin with camps. It began with words. With laws. With people looking the other way. It happened step by step, so small that by the time people realized what was happening, it was too late.

That's why I tell my story. So that people will pay attention. So that they will understand how easily rights can be taken away, how quickly a society can turn against you.

It happens slowly,
until one day,
you wake up and
the world you knew is gone.

- JEANETTE -

Ginette: Were they crying there?

Esther: No, I don't think so.

Ginette: Anyway, we're not crying anymore.

Holocaust Glossary for Educational Use

(With integrated terms for testimony context)

Anti-Jewish Laws: A series of discriminatory laws enacted by Nazi Germany and its collaborators between 1933 and 1945 to isolate and persecute Jews. These laws gradually stripped Jews of their civil, economic, and human rights — excluding them from schools, professions, and public life, and preparing the ground for deportation and extermination.

Appelplatz: German for "roll call square", the place in concentration camps where prisoners were forced to stand, often for hours, to be counted under extreme conditions.

Auschwitz: The largest Nazi concentration and extermination camp, located in occupied Poland. More than 1.1 million people were murdered there, most of them Jews.

Beaune-la-Rolande: A French internment camp, used by the Vichy regime to detain Jews — including children — before their deportation to Auschwitz and other camps.

Bergen-Belsen: A Nazi concentration camp in Germany where many died from starvation, disease, and mistreatment. It is where Anne Frank and her sister Margot died in 1945.

Birkenau: Also known as Auschwitz II, the part of Auschwitz designed for extermination. It contained the gas chambers and crematoria used to murder hundreds of thousands.

Buchenwald: One of the largest and most notorious concentration camps in Germany, where political prisoners, Jews, and other persecuted groups were subjected to forced labor, torture, and death.

Buna: A subcamp of Auschwitz, also known as Monowitz, where prisoners performed forced labor for IG Farben under brutal conditions, with little food or rest.

Death march: Forced marches of prisoners over long distances, typically during the final months of the war, as the Nazis evacuated camps ahead of advancing Allied forces. Prisoners were often shot if they could not keep up.

Drancy: A transit camp located near Paris, used as a holding center before Jews were deported to extermination camps in the East.

Hôtel Lutetia: A hotel in Paris that served as a reception center for survivors returning from the camps at the end of the war. Families would wait there in hopes of finding loved ones.

Kapo: The kapo, a prisoner chosen by the Nazis to supervise the others, beat us with a stick if we didn't move fast enough.

Klaus Barbie: A high-ranking Nazi SS officer, known as the "Butcher of Lyon" for his role in torturing resistance members and deporting Jewish children. He was convicted of crimes against humanity in 1987.

Kommando: A Kommando was a work unit within a Nazi concentration or extermination camp. Prisoners were divided into Kommandos and forced to perform labor — sometimes inside the camp (cleaning, construction, maintenance) and sometimes outside (factories, mines, or other sites). Conditions were brutal, and many prisoners did not survive the work.

Kristallnacht: "The Night of Broken Glass", a state-sponsored pogrom that took place on November 9–10, 1938. Synagogues were burned, Jewish businesses were destroyed, and thousands of Jews were arrested across Nazi Germany and Austria.

Mein Kampf: "My Struggle", the book written by Adolf Hitler while in prison in 1924. It outlines his anti-Semitic ideology and vision for Germany, and later became central to Nazi propaganda.

Mengele: Dr. Josef Mengele, the SS physician at Auschwitz who selected prisoners for the gas chambers and conducted horrific medical experiments, particularly on twins and children.

October 7 Revolt: An uprising by members of the Sonderkommando at Auschwitz-Birkenau on October 7, 1944. Prisoners blew up one of the crematoria using explosives smuggled from a munitions factory by female inmates. The revolt was brutally suppressed, and most participants were killed, but it remains a powerful symbol of resistance within the camp.

OSE (Œuvre de Secours aux Enfants): A Jewish humanitarian organization in France that worked courageously to save thousands of Jewish children during the Holocaust by hiding them with non-Jewish families and in rural homes.

Pithiviers: A French internment camp, like Beaune-la-Rolande, where Jews were imprisoned before being deported to extermination camps.

Sonderkommando: Groups of mostly Jewish prisoners forced to work in the extermination camps, handling the bodies of those killed in the gas chambers and operating the crematoria. They were regularly executed and replaced to eliminate witnesses.

SS: The SS, the Nazi soldiers who ran the camps with brutal authority, would scream at us during roll call, even when we stood perfectly still.

Vel' d'Hiv' (Vélodrome d'Hiver): An indoor sports stadium in Paris, used during the mass roundup of Jews in July 1942. Over 13,000 Jews, including more than 4,000 children, were held there before being sent to Drancy and then deported.

Yellow Star: A yellow six-pointed Star of David badge that Jews were forced to wear on their clothing in Nazi-occupied Europe to mark and segregate them. The word "Jew" was often printed in the center. The badge became a symbol of humiliation, persecution, and resistance.

To watch freely our feature length **documentary film "The Last Ones of Auschwitz"** scan here.

LES
DERNIERS
THE**LAST**
ONES_

@lesderniers_thelastones
@Les_Derniers
@LesDerniers.org
@LesDerniers
@lesderniers.org
thelastones.org
thelastones.education

www.ingramcontent.com/pod-product-compliance
Lightning Source LLC
LaVergne TN
LVHW010638110826
845149LV00014B/2878
* 9 7 9 8 9 9 3 6 1 8 6 0 9 *